R&T Discovery

Step 2

The British Isles

Derek Sellen

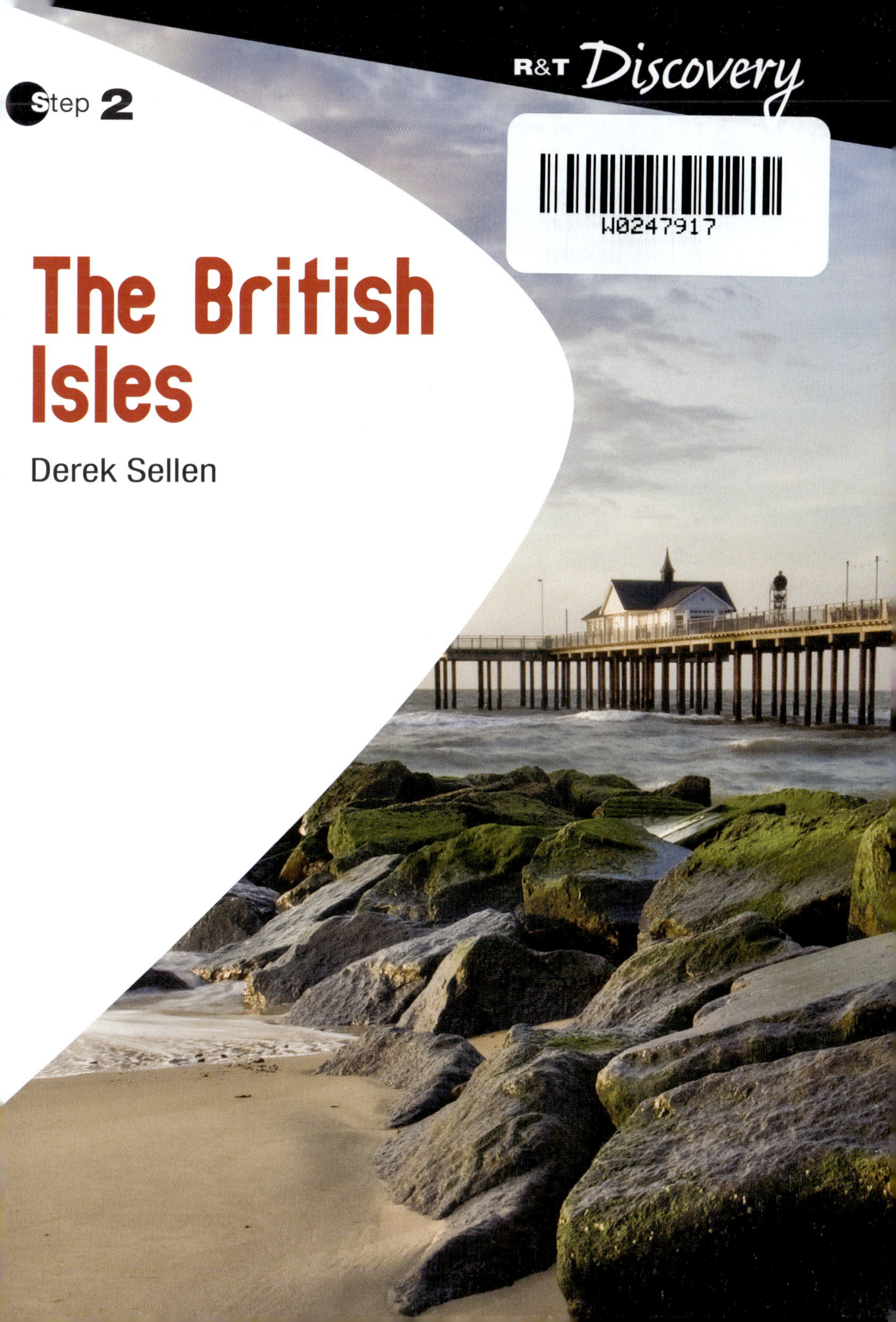

Editors: Joanna Burgess, Michela Bruzzo
Design and art direction: Nadia Maestri
Computer graphics: Maura Santini
Picture research: Laura Lagomarsino

First edition: January 2011

Picture credits
Cideb Archive; Chris Jackson / Getty Images: 10; De Agostini Pictures Library: 20t; Alex Wong / Getty Images: 22; De Agostini Pictures Library: 23, 24; Getty Images: 28; Hulton Archive / Srtinger / Getty Images: 29; Getty Images: 30; Tips Images: 32cb; Joe Fox / Getty Images: 35; Paul O'Driscoll / Getty Images: 36t, Ytoyoda / Creative Commons Attribution – Share Alike 2.0: 36b; De Agostini Pictures Library: 40b; Tips Images: 41; ©Bettmann / CORBIS: 42; Andreas Rentz / Getty Images: 44; Tips Images: 48cl; Christopher Lee / Getty Images: 49; Camera Press / Contrasto: 51tr; Cattherine Karnow/ Corbis: 52t; De Agostini Pictures Library: 62tr; Getty Images: 62bl; Peter Purdy / Getty Images: 63; Getty Images: 64; Christopher Furlong / Getty Images: 65; Webphoto: 68; ©20TH CENTURY FOX – Album / Album / Contrasto: 69; ©SONY PICTURES CLASSICS – HESSION / Contrasto: 70; ©TOUCHSTONE PICTURES – Album / Contrasto: 71; Jakubaszek/Getty Images: 76; De Agostini Pictures Library: 78; John Gichigi / Getty Images: 86b; Tips Images: 87

We would be happy to receive your comments and suggestions, and give you any other information concerning our material.
info@blackcat-cideb.com
blackcat-cideb.com

The Publisher is certified by
CISQCERT
in compliance with the UNI EN ISO 9001:2008 standards for the activities of «Design and production of educational materials»
(certificate no. 02.565)

Printed in Italy by Italgrafica, Novara

Contents

The text is recorded in full.

n. track **end** These symbols indicate the beginning and end of the passages linked to the listening activities.

1 ACTIVITIES

Before you read

1 Vocabulary

Use each word in the box once to fill the gaps in sentences 1-6. Use a dictionary to help you.

accent citizen dialect equator nation saint

1 The people in some parts of the UK have a special .... They use lots of local words and phrases when they speak English.
2 The people in some cities have a local ....
3 A ...... is a person who did many good things in his or her life. The abbreviation (short form) is 'St': for example, St George.
4 Scotland is a separate ...... from England.
5 I am English. I am a ...... of the UK.
6 The ...... is a line on a map that runs around the middle of the Earth.

2 A stereotype is a typical idea of something or somebody. Label these pictures of stereotypes with:

A an American **B** a Scottish person **C** a billionaire

3 What's the difference?

Read quickly through the first section of Chapter One. Then match A-C with 1-3 below.

A The British Isles **B** Great Britain **C** The United Kingdom

1 England, Wales, Scotland and Northern Ireland
2 England, Wales and Scotland
3 England, Wales, Scotland, Ireland (the Republic of Ireland and Northern Ireland), including all the small islands around them

CHAPTER **ONE**

The British Isles

What's the difference between The British Isles, Great Britain and the United[1] Kingdom? Even some British people can't answer that question!

What are they?

track 02

'The British Isles' is a geographical description. We use it to describe England, Wales, Scotland and Ireland, including both Northern Ireland and the Republic of Ireland. In other words the British Isles are the two biggest islands, Great Britain and Ireland, and all the small islands around them.

The United Kingdom is made up of four parts: England, Wales, Scotland and Northern Ireland. On their passports, British people are citizens of the 'United Kingdom of Great Britain and Northern Ireland'. 'British' is the adjective to describe the United Kingdom. The southern part of Ireland, known as the Republic of Ireland or Eire, is an independent nation.

1. **United** : joined together.

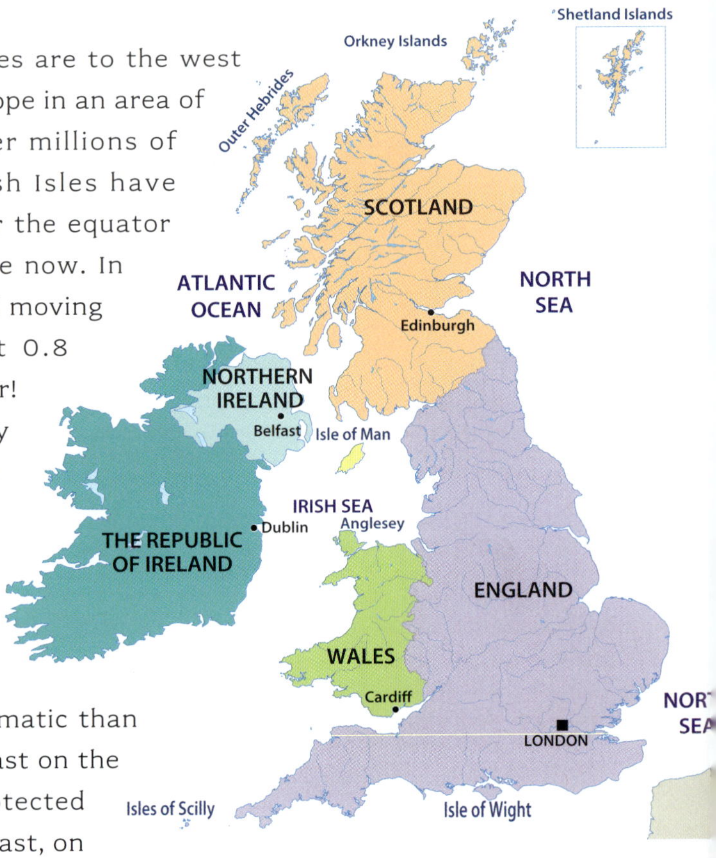

The British Isles are to the west of the rest of Europe in an area of shallow sea. Over millions of years, the British Isles have moved from near the equator to where they are now. In fact, they are still moving north, at about 0.8 centimetres a year!

There are many geographical differences within the British Isles. The Atlantic coast on the west is more dramatic than the North Sea coast on the east and less protected than the south coast, on the English Channel. The mountains of Wales and Scotland are different from the hills of many parts of England. There are very big cities and small villages and even areas where very few people live.

There are more than a thousand small islands. The most well-known are: the Scilly Isles to the south-west; the Isle of Wight to the south; Anglesey off the coast of Wales; the Isle of Man between England and Ireland; the Hebrides, a group of islands off the west coast of Scotland; and Orkney and Shetland to the north of Scotland. The Channel Islands are near the coast of France but they are part of the British Isles. Jersey, Guernsey, Alderney and Sark are the main Channel Islands.

Flags and symbols

Most people know the Union Flag, which is informally called the Union Jack by almost everybody. It's the British flag, which the United Kingdom team carries at the Olympics, for example. It's actually made up of three national flags. One of these is the English flag, a red cross — the cross of St George — on a white background. That's the flag you see when England play sports like football as a separate nation. The Scottish flag, the flag of St Andrew, is a diagonal white cross on a blue background. The third flag is the flag of St Patrick of Ireland, a diagonal red cross on white. When you put the three flags together, you get a red, white and blue flag, the Union Jack.

Wales has its own flag, with a red dragon on it. It isn't included in the Union Flag because the English conquered [2] Wales in the thirteenth century. When the Union Flag was created, people thought that Wales was simply a part of England, so it was represented by the English flag. Each country of the British Isles has its own symbol. England's symbol is the **red rose**. The national saint is **St George** and 23rd April is his saint's day. The **thistle** or the **Scottish bluebell** are often symbols of Scotland. **St Andrew**'s day is 30th November. **St David** is the saint of Wales

2. **conquered** : took by fighting.

and his day is 1st March. The **daffodil** and sometimes the **leek** are symbols of Wales. The **shamrock** is the national symbol of Ireland. **St Patrick**'s day is 17th March and Irish people all over the world celebrate it with the Saint Patrick Day's Parade. In the parade, people wear green, the national colour of Ireland, and march through the streets with music and celebrate.

A place of many languages

Almost everybody in the British Isles speaks English but it's not the only language. If you go to Wales you will see television programmes, notices and road signs in Welsh and hear people speaking it. About 600,000 people speak Welsh there. In Scotland, some people speak Gaelic, especially in the Highlands, and in Ireland, Gaelic or 'Erse' is sometimes used: about 500,000 people in Ireland speak Gaelic everyday. The people are proud of their national languages, which all come from the Celtic language.

These Celtic languages are very different from English. For example: 'How are you?' is 'Shwmae' in Welsh and 'Ciamar a tha thu?' in Gaelic.

'Wales' is 'Cymru' in Welsh and 'Scotland' is 'Alba' in Gaelic.

There are other languages which very few people speak. In Cornwall, in the south-west of England, only a few hundred people speak Cornish. On the Isle of Man, an ancient language known as Manx is used on special occasions.

You will hear lots of other languages, especially in big cities. People who have come to the British Isles from India, Pakistan and Bangladesh may speak Hindi, Punjabi or Bengali, for example.

As well as different languages, you will hear many different accents and dialects. People in Liverpool have a different accent from people in Birmingham, Leeds, Glasgow, Cardiff, London or Manchester, which is near Liverpool. In Newcastle, in the north-east of England, there is a dialect known as 'Geordie'. It has several special words: if the people want to call someone 'darling' or 'honey', they use the word 'hinny': "I love you, my hinny."

Stereotypes

When you think of people from the British Isles what type of people do you imagine? In the past, foreigners imagined the typical English man as a person who carried an umbrella and a briefcase and wore a black suit and a bowler hat. But today, many people see a football hooligan [3] or a pop singer as the typical English person.

Many people imagine that the typical Scottish person has red hair, wears a kilt and plays the bagpipes. He or she speaks with a strong accent and is very careful with his or her money. People think that the typical Welsh person loves rugby and singing and talks too much. They imagine that it always rains in Wales and that most Welsh people are sheep farmers. The typical Irish person drinks Guinness (a strong black Irish beer) and likes telling stories.

3. **hooligan** : someone who fights or behaves very badly in public.

Seamus Heaney.

But are these stereotypes true? For example, some people believe that the English have a big breakfast every day; but in fact most English people have a quick uncooked breakfast. There are lots of jokes about the stupid Irish. But for a small nation, Ireland has a very high number of Nobel Prize winners and great writers. Perhaps you think that it is very difficult to understand a Scottish accent. But the accent of the people in Edinburgh is often voted the most pleasant.

The four nations

Do the Scottish, Welsh and Irish hate the English? Do the Northern Irish hate the Southern Irish? Do the English think that they are the best people in the British Isles?

No. But it is true that there have been problems between the different nations. When there are sports matches between these countries, there is a special excitement. Recently, the devolution of power inside the United Kingdom has begun. Devolution means that the people of Scotland, Wales and Northern Ireland make more political decisions themselves instead of the Parliament in Westminster, London.

How does this work? Since 1998, there has been a new Scottish Parliament in Edinburgh. The members can vote on Scottish issues but London still decides on national policies. The Scottish Nationalist[4] Party (the SNP) is popular in Scotland and

4. **Nationalist** : wanting to be a free, independent country.

wants an independent Scotland. In 2007 the SNP became the largest party in the Scottish Parliament but in the UK elections in 2010 they only got six representatives in the UK Parliament. In Wales there is a National Assembly of Wales and in Northern Ireland there is also an Assembly, but sometimes it can't meet because it is difficult for the different religious and political groups to work together.

The Isle of Man has its own ancient parliament, called the Tynwald, and does not even belong to the European Union. The Tynwald is one of the oldest ruling bodies in the world. Some of its members want the Isle of Man to be independent. The Channel Islands have their own 'States', which are like small parliaments and can pass laws.

Parliament building in Edinburgh.

Parliament, Dublin.

The Republic of Ireland or Eire is an independent nation. It has its own parliament, known as the Houses of Oireachtas in Dublin. Both Eire and the UK are in the European Union but Eire uses the euro as its currency while the UK has kept the pound.

The nations of the British Isles have a long and often exciting history. They are proud of their individual identities but at the same time their culture and politics are very similar to one another. In the later chapters, we will look at each nation in more detail.

The text and **beyond**

PET

1 Comprehension check

Decide if each sentence (1-8) is correct or incorrect. If it is correct, mark A. If it is not correct, mark B.

		A	B
1	The Republic of Ireland is part of the United Kingdom.	☐	☐
2	The British Isles are changing their position little by little.	☐	☐
3	The Union Jack is made up of the Irish, Scottish and English flags.	☐	☐
4	In Wales, people used to speak Welsh but now it is used very little.	☐	☐
5	People in one city often have a different accent from those in other UK cities.	☐	☐
6	Most English people have a big breakfast every day.	☐	☐
7	In Eire, you pay for things using Irish pounds.	☐	☐

2 Vocabulary

Look at the definitions of some words from Chapter One. Can you complete them?

1 something which people might carry to represent a nation — a f..................

2 a flower or other thing which represents a nation — a s..................

3 the place where political decisions are made — P ....

4 the process of giving some independent power to parts of a country — d.....................

5 a language which not many people speak — a m .... language

6 a local pronunciation of a language — an a ....

Think about your own country. Can you describe 1? What is 2? Where is 3? Is there 4 in your country? Are there any 5s? Do people from different cities have different 6s? What are some of the stereotypes about people from your country?

Many different local accents have developed.

We use the Present Perfect for the following different reasons:

A for an action that happened at an unspecified time in the past

B for an action or state that began in the past and has continued until now

C for a recent action with an effect in the present

3 Present Perfect Simple

Complete 1-5 by putting the verbs in brackets in the Present Perfect Simple form. Then write the reason (A-C) for using it.

0 [B] Many different local accents ...have developed... (*develop*)

1 [ ] The Tynwald .... for hundreds of years. (*exist*)

2 [ ] The stereotype of a typical English person .... since the 1950s. (*change*)

3 [ ] People .... the Union Jack upside down by mistake. (*fly*)

4 [ ] Recently, there .... devolution in the UK, so now there is a Scottish Parliament. (*be*)

5 [ ] Many Irish people .... a Nobel Prize. (*win*)

PET 4 Sentence transformation

Here are some sentences about the coast of the British Isles. For each question, complete the second sentence so that it means the same as the first. Use no more than three words.

0 Britain has a very long coastline.
The coastline of Britain ...is very long... .

1 Many sea battles have taken place around the British Isles.
There .... many sea battles around the British Isles.

2 Orkney is closer to the Scottish mainland than Shetland.
Shetland .... the Scottish mainland than Orkney.

3 The English Channel is the calmest stretch of sea.
The English Channel .... any other stretch of sea.

4 In 1987, a hurricane damaged the coastline.
In 1987, the coastline .... a hurricane.

Before you read

1 Vocabulary

Use a dictionary, if necessary, to help you match the people in the box to the sentences.

archaeologist	**archbishop**	**duke**	**invader**
pilgrim	**Pope**	**priest**	**sailor**

1 I study places where there were cities or important buildings in the past. ....

2 I am the leader of the Roman Catholic church. ....

3 I work on boats and ships and travel across the sea. ....

4 I go to other countries and fight because I want to have power in their country. ....

5 I go on a journey to a special place for religious reasons. ....

6 I am the most important person in the Church of England. ....

7 I come from an important, old family and I have a high position in the country. ....

8 You can find me in a church on a Sunday morning. ....

2 **Now match the words 1-3 with the pictures A-C.**

1 a warrior   2 a knight   3 a druid

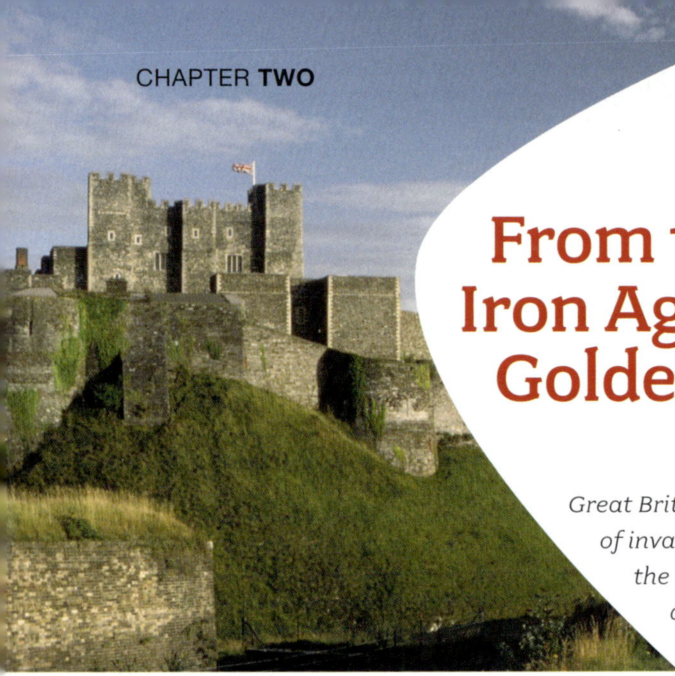

CHAPTER TWO

From the Iron Age to the Golden Age[1]

Great Britain has a long history of invasions, from the Celts and the Romans to the Vikings and the Normans.

BCE = before common era
CE = Common Era
BC = Before Christ
AD = Anno Domini

Ancient Mysteries

track 03

Stonehenge is a mysterious group of huge standing stones. Archaeologists believe that it was built around 2500 BCE,[2] although the first work at the site was done even earlier, in 3100 BCE. That is 5000 years ago! The builders used two types of stone, the 'bluestones' and 'Sarsen' stones. The Sarsen stones

1. **The Golden Age** : a period of history when a country is very successful.
2. **BCE** : we use BCE (before the Common Era) and CE (Common Era) to talk about dates before and after the year 0. For example, the date 1000 BCE is about 3,000 years ago.

come from near Stonehenge and each one weighed twenty-five tons. However, the bluestones came from nearly 400 kilometres away. But how did they transport the bluestones so far and how did they lift the stones into a standing position?

A third mystery is: what was the purpose? Many people believe that the stones were placed in this way to look at the movement of the stars and the sun and moon. It was probably also important for the religion of the people who built it.

There is another famous ancient monument near Stonehenge – the stone ring at Avebury, about 60km east of Bristol. This is the largest stone circle in the world and it is near Silbury Hill, the tallest man-made hill in Europe. There are also standing stones in many places in Ireland.

The Celts

The Celts lived in Britain in the Iron Age from around 600 BCE. They came from Central Europe and we know about the Celts from the objects which archaeologists have found and from some Greek and Roman writers, who tell us that the Celts loved gold and fighting. Their priests were called Druids and had great power in Celtic society.

We also know about the Celts from the 'bog bodies'. Bogs are areas of wet land; if a body is buried in a bog, it is kept in good condition, perhaps for centuries. In England in 1984 some workers discovered 'Lindow Man'. Lindow Man was killed in the first century CE, so it is a 2000-year-old murder mystery. Some people think that he was killed by the Druids for religious reasons. You can see Lindow Man in the British Museum in London.

A warrior queen

In 55 BCE, Julius Caesar [3] invaded Britain. The Celts were great warriors but the Romans had better organisation and defeated [4] them. Caesar returned in 54 BCE. This time, the Roman army crossed the River Thames but Caesar left after the Britons agreed to give money to the Romans.

In CE 43, nearly a hundred years later, the Roman Emperor Claudius sent another army of about 50,000 men to Britain. This time the Romans stayed and Britain became part of the Roman Empire. [5]

Camulodunum, now called Colchester, in the East of England was the first capital. But in CE 60 there was a revolution [6] against the Romans. Boudicca was queen of the Iceni tribe and a warrior too. She hated the Romans because they were very cruel to her and her daughters. Her army attacked and destroyed Colchester and then burnt Londinium (now London). But the Romans won the next battle and Boudicca killed herself. The Romans later controlled most of Britain.

3. **Julius Caesar** : a very important Roman leader.
4. **defeated** : won a fight, a competition or in a war.
5. **Empire** : a group of countries under the control of a powerful country, for example the Roman Empire included large parts of Europe, Asia and northern Africa.
6. **revolution** : a fight against the powerful people in a country.

The Roman occupation

Londinium now became the new Roman capital. The Romans also created many other towns. If a modern British city name ends in *-cester* or *-caster* or *-chester*, it was originally a Roman camp because the Romans called them *castra*. Chester, Manchester, Leicester, Lancaster and Gloucester are all examples of Roman cities. The Romans improved the services in the country, and built straight roads such as Watling Street, which runs from Dover in the south-east of England to Wales. Today it is still an important road in Britain.

But they did not control Scotland. In CE 122, the Emperor Hadrian visited Britain and decided to build a wall across the north of England to defend Roman Britain against the Picts in Scotland. The Picts were different Celtic groups who lived in Scotland. Hadrian's Wall is 117 kilometres long and goes from Wallsend on the North Sea in the east to Bowness on the Irish Sea in the west. It was very strong and large parts of it are still there today.

The King Buried in a Ship

In CE 410, the Romans left Britain. They went to defend Rome against the barbarians, who were not in the Roman Empire, and left Britain without any protection. Soon, invaders arrived from north-west Europe and took control of the country. These were the Anglo-Saxons and the Jutes. We know a lot about them because archaeologists have found many objects from their times.

In the 7th century, a king was buried at Sutton Hoo in the south-east of England. His people pulled a long wooden ship up a hill and buried him in it. They buried many gold and silver objects with him, including a helmet. The ship was discovered in 1939 and you can see these magnificent objects in the British Museum.

More recently, in July 2009, another collection of Anglo-Saxon objects was found in Staffordshire in north-west England. These objects are known as the 'Staffordshire Hoard' and are the largest discovery of objects from the time of the Anglo-Saxons. The British Art Fund bought them for £3.3 million.

The Anglo-Saxons and the Vikings

The Anglo-Saxons had a big influence on England; in fact the name England comes from 'Angle-land'. They divided the country into five kingdoms: [7] Northumbria, Mercia, Wessex, Kent and Anglia. The names we use today for different parts of the country come from this period, such as Essex, Sussex, Wessex. Most of the basic words in the English language also come from the Anglo-Saxons, such as *mother, father, woman, day, night, bed*, *go* and *house*. Some of the days of the week come from the names of Anglo-Saxon gods.

In CE 597, a monk called Augustine came to England. He was sent by the Pope and he slowly told people about the Christian religion all over the country. You can still see Anglo-Saxon stone churches in Britain today.

Alfred the Great.

7. **kingdoms** : areas under the control of a king or queen.

From CE 800, Vikings from Denmark and Norway began to attack Britain. The most famous Saxon king was Alfred the Great; he fought against the Vikings. Although he won, he allowed them to live in the area around York. They also controlled the north-west of Scotland. But little by little, Wessex, in the south-west of England, became the most important kingdom and Saxon kings ruled England.

The Normans

1066 is the best-known date in British history. A duke from Normandy, on the north coast of France said that he was the real king of England and invaded it. The Saxon king, Harold, was fighting in the north but he returned quickly and there was a great battle at Hastings. Harold was killed, the Normans won and William became the first Norman king, called William the Conqueror.

The Normans built many castles and cathedrals. French became the language of the rulers for about 300 years. The Normans created a feudal system, where they were the lords and the Saxons were the serfs. With this system the lords owned the land, animals and buildings and the serfs were workers who had to work on the land for the lords.

The Middle Ages

In the Middle Ages, both the king and the church had great power. This sometimes led to problems. For example, King Henry II argued with Thomas Becket, the Archbishop of Canterbury, and, as a result, Becket was killed by some of Henry's knights in 1170. But Henry was sorry for the murder and for centuries pilgrims came to visit Becket's tomb. [8]

There was also a fight for power between the kings and the rich men in England. The King wanted to collect money to pay for his wars but the rich men didn't like this. They invaded London and in 1215 they made King John sign the Magna Carta, a document which limited the king's power and created a strong parliament. The Magna Carta is very important because it introduced shared power between the king and the people.

In 1348, the Black Death came to England. This was a terrible disease which passed from one person to another quickly and killed nearly half of the 5-6 million people living there.

Throughout the Middle Ages, there were important wars. In 1337, the 'Hundred Years War' between England and France began when King Edward III of England said that he should also be King of France. He invaded France and for the following 116 years there were wars between England and France. During this war, a young woman, Joan of Arc, [9] fought for the French and, although the English caught her and burned her, she helped the French to win because she was so brave. At the end of the war, England had lost all its land in France except Calais.

8. **tomb** : the place where a person is buried after they die.
9. **Joan of Arc** : a national heroine of France and a catholic saint. She led the French army to many victories during the Hundred Years' War. She was then burned at the stake by an ecclesiastical court.

Later, there was a war in England between two leading families, the House of Lancaster and the House of York. Both 'houses' wanted someone from their family to be King of England. It was called the War of the Roses because the symbol of Lancaster was a red rose and the symbol of York was a white rose. It began in 1455 and ended in 1485, when Henry Tudor, from the House of Lancaster, defeated Richard III, from the House of York, at the Battle of Bosworth. Richard was the last English king who was killed in a battle.

Joan of Arc, miniature painting, Antoine Du Four, 1505.

The Tudor period

Henry Tudor became King Henry VII, the first Tudor king. He created the 'Tudor rose', which joined the red and the white rose. It was a symbol of peace between Lancaster and York.

His son, Henry VIII, is famous for having six wives. King Henry first married Catherine of Aragon but wanted to divorce [10] her so that he could marry Anne Boleyn. He wanted to have a son to become king after him. When the Pope didn't allow the divorce, Henry separated the English church from Rome. Two of Henry's wives were beheaded [11] — Anne Boleyn and Catherine Howard.

10. **divorce** : end of marriage.
11. **beheaded** : their heads were cut off.

The Spanish Armada against England in 1588.

Henry had two daughters. Mary had a Roman Catholic mother, Catherine of Aragon. When she became queen, she returned England to the Roman Catholic church. People call her 'Bloody Mary' because many Protestants were killed during her reign.[12] But when Mary died, her sister, Elizabeth, became queen. Elizabeth's mother, Anne Boleyn, was a Protestant, and so Elizabeth started the Protestant Church of England again.

Elizabeth's reign was a golden age for England. Many important things happened and England became rich and powerful and successful. There were many famous writers; for example, William Shakespeare wrote his plays and poems during this time. English sailors such as Francis Drake explored the world and challenged the power of Spain. When the Spanish tried to attack England in 1588, their fleet of ships were defeated. England became the main Protestant nation in Europe.

12. **reign** : the period when a king or queen is in power.

The text and **beyond**

1 Comprehension check

Put these events into chronological order (= order of time). Write 1 for the earliest and 10 for the latest. The first one has been done for you.

A ☐ 'Lindow Man' was discovered.
B ☐ Henry VIII married six times.
C ☐ Queen Mary's sister became queen.
D [0] Stonehenge was built.
E ☐ The War of the Roses took place.
F ☐ Boudicca fought against the Romans.
G ☐ The period of Tudor power began.
H ☐ The Saxons and Vikings were powerful in Britain.
I ☐ An English king was killed in battle.
J ☐ Hadrian's Wall was built.
K ☐ The Normans arrived in Britain.

2 Days of the week

The Anglo-Saxons gave the days the names of their gods. The Romans also did this. Write the modern name of the day of the week next to each god.

The day of:

0 Tiwe, the god of war ......Tuesday.....
1 the sun ....
2 Woden, the chief god ....
3 Frigg, the goddess of love ....
4 the moon ....
5 Saturn, a Roman god ....
6 Thor/Thunor, the god of thunder ....

The text and beyond

3 Vocabulary

Replace the underlined parts in 1-5 with verbs from the box.

~~apologise~~	control	defeat	discover	know as	observe

0 King Henry said sorry for the murder of Becket.
........King Henry apologised for the murder of Becket............... .

1 Henry Tudor won the battle against Richard III

2 The disease was called 'the Black Death'.

3 The Vikings had power in north-west Scotland.

4 'Lindow Man' was found by some workers.

5 Perhaps they used Stonehenge to look at the stars..

England had lost all of its land in France...

We often use the Past Perfect form of a verb to show that an action happened earlier in the past than another action in the Past Simple.
E.g. After they **had killed** King Harold, the Normans **ruled** England.
= They **killed** Harold first and **then** they ruled England.

4 The Past Perfect

In 1-4 below, use one of the verbs in brackets in the Past Perfect form and the other verb in the Past Simple form.

0 Bronze Age people ....built........ Stonehenge after they had brought stones from other areas of Britain. (*build, bring*)

1 Claudius .... an army nearly 100 years after Julius Caesar .... the British Isles. (*send, invade*)

2 Boudicca .... a revolution because the Romans .... her and her daughters badly. (*begin, treat*)

3 After the Romans .... Britain, invaders .... from Europe. (*leave, arrive*)

4 French .... the language of the rulers after the Normans .... King Harold. (*become, defeat*)

Before you read

1 Vocabulary

Use a dictionary to help you write the correct word from the box.

a famine	a multi-racial society	a mutiny	a plot

1 When soldiers fight against their officers, it is ....
2 When there is not enough food and people are dying, it is ....
3 When people from different races, with different religions and different customs, live together in one society, it is ....
4 When people make a secret plan, it is ....

Now match the verbs in the box with the definitions 1-5.

to ban	to colonise	to dominate	to manufacture	to rebuild

1 to forbid, not to allow ....
2 to make in a factory, using machines ....
3 to go to live in another country and to take control ....
4 to use your power to control other people ....
5 to build again ....

2 Listening

track 04

Listen to the first part of Chapter Three twice. Write a year in the spaces in sentences 1-4.

1 In .... Guy Fawkes tried to kill the King.
2 In .... Charles I became king.
3 In .... a war began in England.
4 In .... Charles I was killed.

CHAPTER **THREE**

From the Gunpowder Plot to Global Warming [1]

The Industrial Revolution changed the way people lived and made Britain rich, but it also created many problems

The Execution [2] of a King

track 04

On 4th November 1605, a man named Guy Fawkes hid under the Houses of Parliament with at least 20 barrels [3] of gunpowder. [4] He and four other men planned to blow up King James I when he opened Parliament the next day. Fawkes was a Roman Catholic and he was angry because he thought that the King's laws were unfair to people of his religion. He had everything he needed — gunpowder, matches, a watch — to kill the most important people in England. But he was arrested on the 5th November in the morning and the King was safe! This was the end of the 'gunpowder plot'.

1. **Global warming** : the idea that the earth is getting warmer because of human activities.
2. **execution** : killing someone because they have done something wrong.
3. **barrels** : wooden containers.
4. **gunpowder** : dangerous chemicals which can cause a big explosion.

Failed Conspirator, Sir John Gilbert, 1754.

When James' son Charles became king in 1625, he wanted the King to be more important than the Government. Some people thought that Charles agreed with the Catholics but the Government wanted a Protestant England. Charles I tried to close Parliament and to govern the country alone.

The Civil War began in 1642. It divided the country between the Royalists, who supported King Charles, and the Parliamentarians, who supported Oliver Cromwell, the Protestant leader. Sometimes families were divided. There were many battles and many people were killed. Finally, Cromwell won and on 30th January, 1649, Charles I was beheaded.

end

Christmas is cancelled

From 1649 to 1660, there was no king or queen in England. Cromwell became 'Lord Protector'. He took an army to Ireland, where they killed many Irish soldiers and sent boys and women as slaves [5] to the Caribbean. He also gave land in Ireland to his Protestant soldiers who came to live in Ireland. Cromwell's actions were the start of the twentieth-century problems between Catholics and Protestants in Ireland. In England, the Protestants banned theatre and were very strict about religion

5. **slaves** : people who work without being paid and belong to their owners.

and how people behaved: women could not wear bright colours or make-up. Christmas was also banned by limiting Christmas celebrations.

Plague, Fire and Revolution

Cromwell died in 1658 and in 1660 Charles II, the dead king's son, became king. He was popular but during his reign there were two terrible events. The first was the 'Great Plague' (1664), when a disease, bubonic plague, killed about 20% of the population of London. The second was the 'Great Fire of London' (1666), which destroyed many buildings in the capital. Parts of London had to be rebuilt; St Paul's Cathedral was among the new churches designed by the famous architect [6] Christopher Wren.

After Charles died, Parliament became unhappy with the new king, James II, who was a Catholic. In 1688, Parliament invited a Dutch Protestant, William of Orange, to invade the country. William was married to James' daughter Mary. James ran away to France and William and Mary became king and queen.

It was not the end of the problem. In 1745, 'Bonnie [7] Prince Charlie', the grandson of James II, took an army from Scotland to Derby in the middle of England. Finally, however, his army lost and he had to escape from Scotland wearing a woman's clothes to hide his identity.

6. **architect** : someone who designs buildings.
7. **Bonnie** : a Scottish word meaning 'handsome' or 'pretty'.

England + Wales + Scotland + Ireland

Anne was another daughter of James II and she became Queen in 1702. During her reign, two political parties developed in Parliament, the Whigs and the Tories. This was the start of the modern British political system. Two important acts [8] were passed by Parliament. The Act of Settlement (1701) said that no Roman Catholic could be king or queen. The Act of Union (1707) said that England and Scotland were one country.

When Anne died without any children, Britain had to look for a Protestant king. This was King George I, who was German and spoke very little English. It was the start of the Georgian Age in Britain. George II, George III and George IV followed. During the reign of George III, Britain lost its colonies in America as a result of the American War of Independence (1775-1783). But the British colonised Australia and British power grew in India during this period.

In 1727, Robert Walpole became the first British prime minister. In 1735, George II gave Walpole a house in London while he was governing the country. That house was 10 Downing Street, where British prime ministers still live today.

In 1801, the government introduced the Act of Union with Ireland. As a result, Britain needed a new flag to join the English, Scottish and Irish flags. This was the Union Jack (see Chapter One).

After Napoleon took power in France at the beginning of the 19th century, Britain and France were at war. Two men became national heroes: Admiral Nelson defeated the

8. **acts** : laws which are made by Parliament.

French at the battle of Trafalgar (1805), and the Duke of Wellington defeated Napoleon's armies at the battle of Waterloo (1815). Nelson's statue in Trafalgar Square and Wellington Arch in London are monuments to remember these heroes.

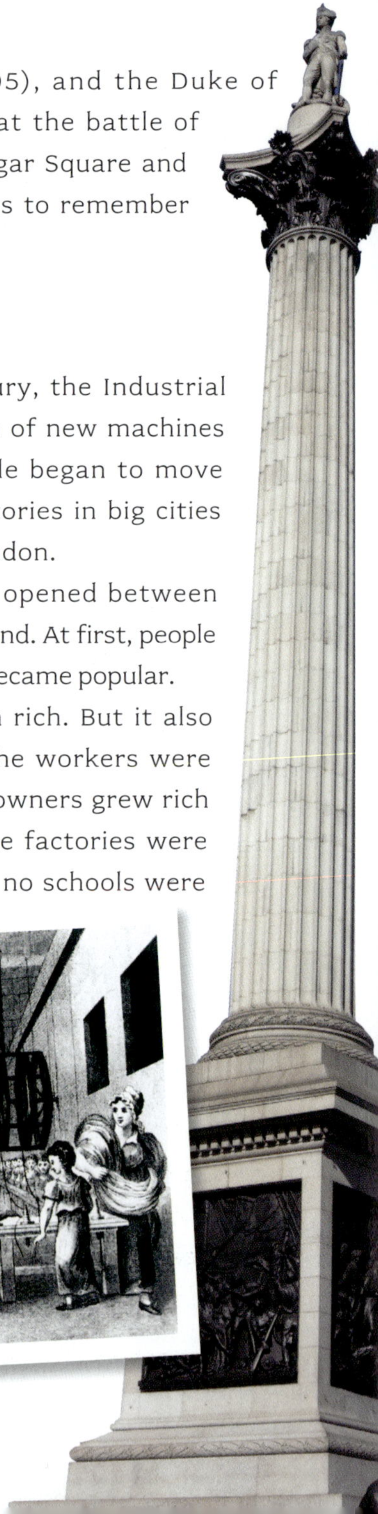

The Industrial Revolution

Towards the end of the eighteenth century, the Industrial Revolution began in Britain. The invention of new machines changed the way that people lived. People began to move from the country to find work in the factories in big cities like Birmingham, Manchester, Leeds or London.

In 1825, the world's first railway was opened between Stockton and Darlington in the north of England. At first, people were afraid of travelling by train but it soon became popular.

The Industrial Revolution made Britain rich. But it also created problems. Living conditions for the workers were very crowded and unhealthy. The factory owners grew rich but the workers were often very poor. The factories were not very safe and children had to work so no schools were created for them.

Coal was the main fuel of the revolution, so children worked in the mines. Some children worked underground for 18 hours each day.

The Victorian Age

In 1834, a young woman, only eighteen years old, became queen of Britain. Later, she became Empress of India. She fell in love with Albert, a German prince, and after his death in 1861, she kept his memory alive. Her face was on the first postage stamps in the world and her statue was placed not only in Britain but in all parts of the British Empire. During her reign, many British men and women such as Charles Dickens, Florence Nightingale, Charles Darwin, Alexander Graham Bell and Lewis Caroll became world-famous. Her name was Victoria.

There were many changes in society: using children as workers became illegal, education became free for everyone and the industrial cities were made safer and healthier. The railway system covered the whole country and there were advances in science. The British Empire grew to include parts of Africa and Asia. Britain dominated the seas with its strong navy [9] and was a centre of world trade.

But Queen Victoria and her government had many problems. From 1845 to 1849 there was the 'Great Potato Famine' in Ireland. Potatoes are just one of many foods that are available for us but the Irish depended on them in the nineteenth century. A disease killed the potato plants and about 1 million Irish people died because they had no food. About another million left Ireland

9. **navy** : the fighting ships and the sailors of a country.

and many of them went to America. The British Government did not do enough to help them. From 1854 to 1856 there was a war with Russia when more than 20,000 British soldiers died. In 1857, Indian soldiers attacked their British officers in the Indian mutiny. Although the British got back control of India, the fighting between the Indians and the British lasted for more than a year. In 2007, the government of India celebrated 150 years since this 'First War of Independence'.

Britain changed greatly during the Victorian Age. At the end of the period, there were electric lights, telephones, the London underground and many things became more modern.

The Twentieth Century

During the twentieth century, Britain went through more changes. The population grew from about forty million to sixty million. The country was involved in two world wars (1914-1918 and 1939-1945), and in other wars too. Technological and scientific progress had a huge effect on life in the United Kingdom and in Ireland in this century. Life expectancy [10] in the United Kingdom increased from about 48 years in 1901 to about 78 years in 2000.

The relationship between Great Britain and Ireland changed. At the start of the century, Ireland was a part of Britain and was governed from London. But many Irish people wanted to be free. In 1919, the Irish War of Independence began and finally, in 1921, the south of Ireland became independent. The people in this part of Ireland were mainly Roman Catholic but the people who lived in the north were mainly Protestant and wanted to remain part of Britain; so Northern Ireland stayed in the United Kingdom. The island of Ireland was divided.

10. **life expectancy** : the average length of people's lives.

Loyalist wall mural, lower Shankill road, on September 22, 2008 in Belfast, Northern Ireland. This mural depicts the Irish myth regarding the red hand of Ulster.

Some Catholic Irish lived in the north and believed that the situation was unfair. They also wanted a united Ireland. This led to a period known as 'the troubles' in Northern Ireland from the late 1960s until 1999. The Irish Republican Army (the IRA) and the British army fought and there were more than 3,500 deaths in this period. In 1998, the 'Good Friday Agreement' [11] was signed and 'the troubles' ended.

After the second world war, countries in the British empire became independent; India and Pakistan in 1947 and African countries such as Kenya, Ghana and Nigeria in the following years. Many of these countries are part of the British Commonwealth, an association of English-speaking countries from the former Empire.

In the 1960s, there was great social change. Teenagers had more freedom, the role of women began to change and the rules of society were relaxed. This was the time of the Beatles and the Rolling Stones and many other successful British music groups. The 1960s are known as 'the swinging sixties'.

The British Isles saw many other important changes in the second half of the twentieth century – it entered the European Community in 1973; Margaret Thatcher was the first British

11. **Good Friday Agreement** : a peace agreement signed between Northern Ireland, the United Kingdom and Ireland.

female prime minister (1979-90); North Sea oil was discovered; the Channel Tunnel, which joins Britain to the rest of Europe, was built; a multi-racial society developed; Scotland, Northern Ireland and Wales became more independent.

Into the Twenty-first Century

Britain continues to change. The Scottish Parliament, the National Assembly for Wales and the Northern Ireland Assembly make those nations more independent. People face the problem of global warming – the British Isles have had some unusual weather and there have been serious floods. From 2008, there have been economic problems in all the nations of the British Isles because of the world recession.[12] A new UK government, with two parties that share power, was elected in 2010. London is getting ready for the Olympics in 2012.

12. **recession** : a bad economic time for business.

Olympic Stadium, London.

The text and **beyond**

1 Comprehension check

Answer the following questions. The first one has been done for you.

WHO AM I?

0 I wanted to kill the King when he was in Parliament. Guy Fawkes

1 I was the King. I wanted to govern without Parliament. ....

2 When I had power, there was no Christmas. ....

3 I designed a great new cathedral after the fire. ....

4 I was King of England but I didn't speak English well. ....

5 I was the first Prime Minister in 10 Downing Street. ....

6 I was a teenage queen. Later, I was an Empress. ....

WHAT IS IT?

7 It is a transport system in London. ....

8 It is a group of countries which used to be part of the British Empire. ....

9 It connects Britain and the rest of Europe. ....

2 Vocabulary

Complete the words in 1-8. You can use a dictionary if you need to. All the words are about politics.

1 the people who decide what the country should do — the g _ v _ _ _ ment

2 the place where these people discuss what to do — P _ _ _ _ _ _ ment

3 this is when the people choose a new '1' — an el _ _ _ ion

4 this is the leader of '1' — the P _ _ _ _ M _ _ _ _ ter

5 this happens when the people fight '1' — a r _ v _ _ _ _ ion

6 these are the people who are in '2' — M _ _ _ ers of P _ _ _ _ _ _ ment

7 this is what you do during '3' — v _ _ _

8 the system where you have '3's — dem _ _ _ _ _ _

3 Irregular verbs

Complete 1-8 with verbs from the box in the Past Simple.

become	fall	fight	grow	take	lose	run	speak	wear

1 James .... away to France and William and Mary .... king and queen.
2 Bonnie Prince Charlie .... an army as far as Derby.
3 Bonnie Prince Charlie .... women's clothes when he escaped.
4 George I .... very little English.
5 After the American War of Independence, Britain .... its colonies in America.
6 Victoria .... in love with Albert.
7 In the twentieth century, the population .... rapidly.
8 The IRA and the British army .... against each other.

4 Prepositions

Read these pairs of sentences. Write a suitable preposition in the gaps to give the sentence the same meaning as the first sentence.

1 Guy Fawkes brought gunpowder.
Guy Fawkes took gunpowder .... him.
2 1642 was the start of the war.
The war began .... 1642.
3 30th January was the date of his death.
Charles died .... 30th January.
4 People thought the trains were dangerous.
People were afraid .... the trains.
5 Life expectancy was 48 years.
People lived .... 48 years on average.
6 The Channel Tunnel joins two countries.
The Channel Tunnel goes .... France and England.

5 Listening

track 05

PET

You will hear a guide talking about an exhibition on the life of Isambard Kingdom Brunel. For each question, fill in the missing information in the numbered space.

EXHIBITION ON THE LIFE OF ISAMBARD KINGDOM BRUNEL

A GREAT (**0**) ..Victorian.. ENGINEER

* He lived from 1806 to (**1**) ....

* He designed and built railways, (**2**) ...., tunnels and ships

* In Bristol docks, you can see his ship, the (**3**) ....

* He also designed two other big steamships, the *Great Western* and the *Great Eastern*

The exhibition runs from (**4**) .... until late summer.

OPENING TIMES: Weekdays: (**5**) .... until 5 p.m.

Weekends: 11 a.m. until (**6**) .... p.m.

PET

6 Writing

An English friend of yours called Rachel helped you to write some homework about the history of the British Isles. Write a card to send to Rachel. In your card, you should:

- thank her for doing this
- say if you got a good mark for your homework
- offer to help her with her homework next time

Write 35-45 words.

Great British Scientists and Inventors

Many scientists, inventors and engineers have come from the British Isles. Here are some questions about a few of them.

Which great scientist believed in magic?

Isaac Newton (1643-1727) studied light, developed new ideas in mathematics, showed that gravity [1] existed and found the three laws of motion. Newton's laws of motion explain, for example, how an aeroplane can fly. There has never been a more important scientist than Newton. But he was also very interested in alchemy, a mixture of magic and chemistry.

Who developed the theory of evolution? [2]

Most people answer '**Charles Darwin**'(1809-1882). Darwin travelled for five years on a ship called *the Beagle* [3] and collected examples of different animals, birds, insects etc. As a result of his discoveries, and many more years of research, he published a book

1. **gravity** : the force that pulls objects towards the earth; things fall because of gravity.
2. **evolution** : the idea that plants and animals etc. develop and change over millions of years.
3. **Beagle** : the name of a type of hunting dog.

called *On the Origin of the Species* [4] in 1859. In this book, he wrote that species have 'evolved' over millions of years.

However, another British man was working in the same area of science. This was **Alfred Russell Wallace** (1823-1913). Like Darwin, he travelled a lot, visiting the Amazon and Malaysia. Wallace developed ideas which were similar to Darwin's and he is also responsible for the theory of evolution. However, Darwin's name is more famous. Darwin is buried in Westminster Abbey while Wallace is buried near a small village church in Broadstone, Dorset.

Who invented nursing?

Is nursing an invention? If it is, the inventor is **Florence Nightingale** (1820-1910). She came from a rich family but she decided not to marry and to be a nurse instead. At this time, the 1840s, nurses were not trained. Florence became famous when she went to Turkey to

4. **species** : a type of animal, bird, insect or plant etc.

Florence Nightingale in the barrack hospital at Scutari, about 1880.

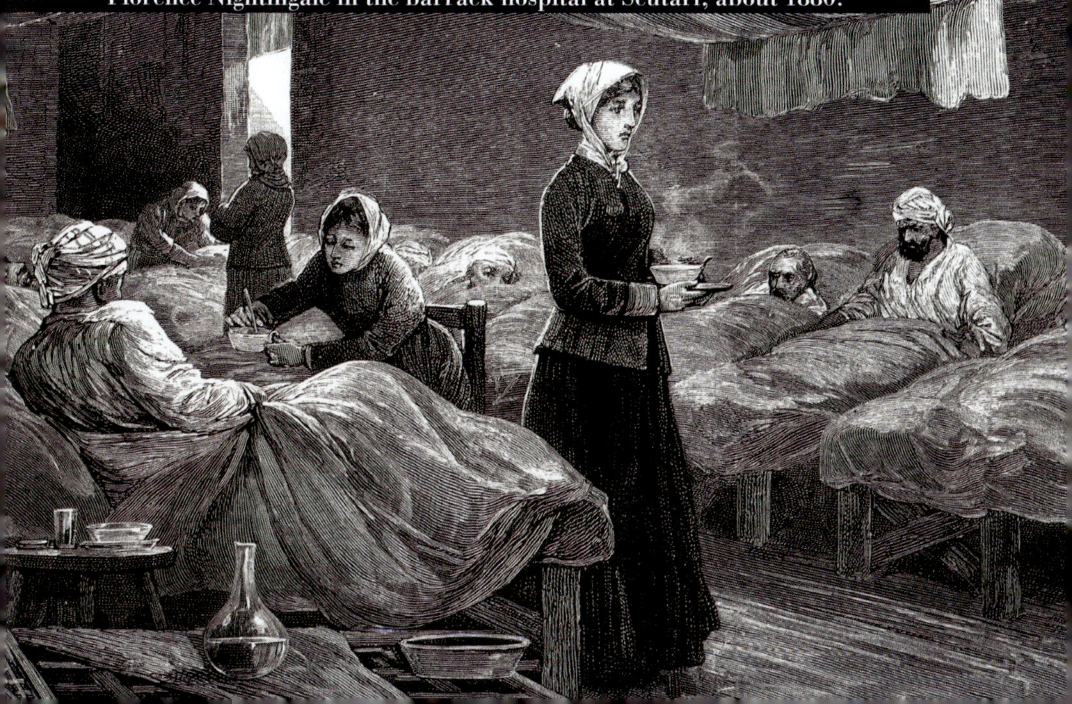

help wounded British soldiers who were fighting in the Crimean war, a war against Russia. They called her 'the lady with the lamp' because she visited the sick soldiers at night carrying a lamp. She also made sure that the conditions were clean and healthy. When she returned, she established training schools for nurses, where they learnt that it was important to have clean hospitals. This was the beginning of today's professional nurses.

Who won the race to invent television?

Even when he was a young child, **John Logie Baird** (1888-1946) liked to invent things. He dreamt of inventing a television, but when he told a newspaper about this, they thought he was mad and were afraid of him! But in 1926 he showed other scientists the world's first successful television. Later, he even produced colour television pictures. However, in the USA, scientists were also inventing a TV system. Finally, the American Marconi system became the basis for today's television.

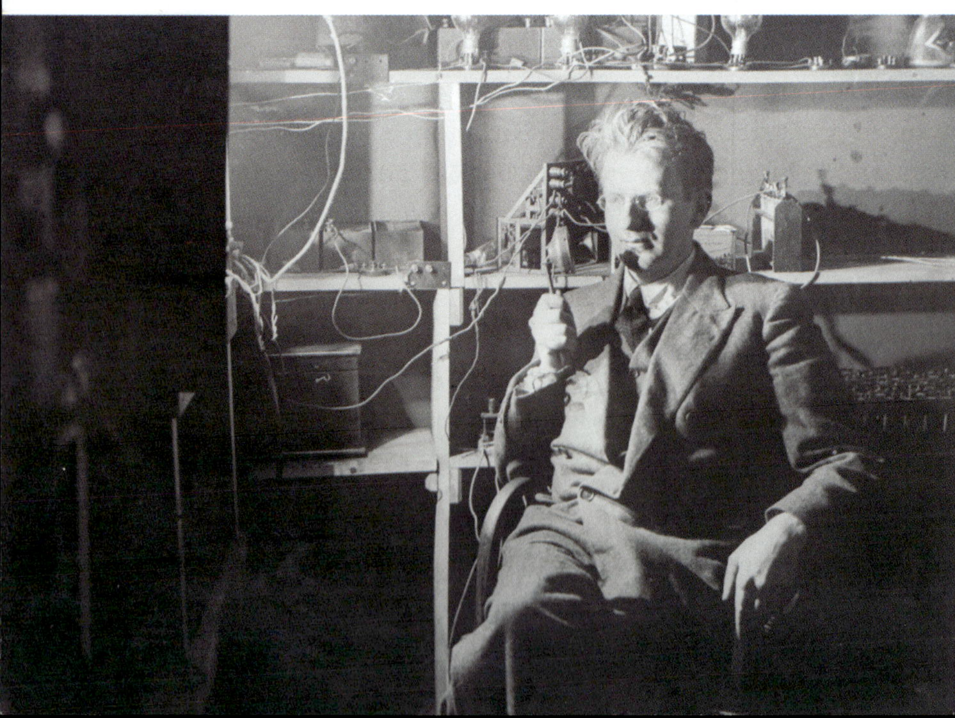

Would you like to have a crater[5] on the moon with your name on it?

William Thomson (1824-1907), who was born in Belfast, gave his name to the Thomson crater on the moon. He was a successful physicist[6] and engineer: for example, he worked on the first transatlantic cable under the ocean from The British Isles to the USA. He made inventions and discoveries in many areas of science. He became **Lord Kelvin** and a 'Kelvin' is a unit of temperature that scientists use – absolute zero is 0 K on the Kelvin scale.

Can a woman be a great scientist?

In 1974, the Nobel Prize committee didn't think so. **Jocelyn Bell Burnell** (born 1943), a female astro-physicist[7] born in Northern Ireland, worked with two male scientists, Hewish and Royle. She discovered important facts about pulsars, special types of stars, and the development of the galaxies, which are large groups of stars and planets. But who got the Nobel Prize? Her male colleagues. Nowadays even NASA (the North American Space Agency) says on their website: 'Pulsars were discovered in late 1967 by graduate student Jocelyn Bell Burnell.' She didn't win the Nobel Prize but she has been honoured in other ways.

5. **crater** : a hole in the surface of the moon.
6. **physicist** : a scientist who studies natural physical laws.
7. **astro-physicist** : a scientist who studies the stars.

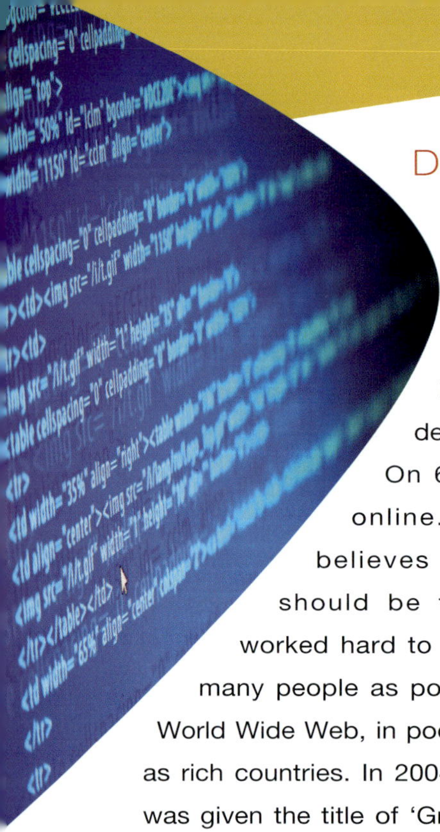

Did the World Wide Web invent itself?

The World Wide Web is now a part of our everyday lives, and so it is easy to forget that somebody invented it. In fact, **Sir Tim Berners-Lee** (born in London in 1955) developed the web between 1980 and 1991. On 6th August 1991, the first website went online. Berners-Lee believes that information should be free and he has worked hard to make sure that as many people as possible can use the World Wide Web, in poor countries as well as rich countries. In 2004, Tim Berners-Lee was given the title of 'Greatest Briton' by a group of judges. He has been given many other awards.

1 Comprehension check

Match the names of the people 1-8 with items A-J.

A	television	F	pulsars
B	nursing	G	the transatlantic cable
C	the worldwide web	H	Malaysia
D	*On the Origin of Species*	I	the laws of motion
E	gravity	J	absolute zero

1	☐ John Logie Baird	5	☐ Alfred Russell Wallace
2	☐ Jocelyn Bell Burnell	6	☐ Florence Nightingale
3	☐ Sir Tim Berners Lee	7	☐ ☐ William Thomson
4	☐ Charles Darwin	8	☐ ☐ Isaac Newton

INTERNET PROJECT

Look again at Charles Darwin. Connect to the Internet and go to www.blackcat-cideb.com. Insert the title or part of the title of the book into our search engine. Open the page for *The British Isles*. Click on the Internet project link. Then answer the following questions.

1. Where can you sometimes see Darwin's face?
2. Which city was named after Darwin? Where is it?
3. Who was Jenny?
4. Did he write his first scientific paper about biology?
5. What percentage of British people believe in evolution?
6. Did Darwin write *On the Origin of Species* for scientists only?
7. Did his father expect him to be famous?
8. What did Darwin study at university? Was he successful?
9. What did Darwin do with his specimen of the lesser rhea?
10. Which islands did he explore?

Charles Darwin 200: Facts : Enjoy England

Register | Login

enjoyEngland The official website for breaks and days out in England

Search enjoyEngland GO

Home | Destinations | Accommodation | Attractions & events | Interests | Buy tickets & days out | Reviews & videos | E-newsletter | Choose language

City breaks | Food & drink | Rural escapes | Heritage & culture | Family fun | Relaxing breaks | Competitions

heritage&Culture

Competitions and offers
City breaks
Food and drink
Rural escapes
Heritage and culture
Family fun
Relaxing breaks

Darwin facts

More

• During the five-year Beagle expedition, Darwin shipped home 1,529 species preserved in spirit and 3,907 labelled skins, bones and other dried specimens.

• Charles Darwin beat Charles Dickens to become the face of the new £10 note in 2000. Apparently his beard makes it hard to reproduce his portrait hair by hair.

• Darwin was voted in the top five greatest Britons by BBC viewers in 2002.

• Darwin is the most frequently featured person on stamps outside the Royal Family.

• Darwin in north Australia was named by two of Darwin's former shipmates who led the Beagle's next voyage. Darwin is now a thriving city and has its own Darwin200 celebrations planned.

• The first ape Darwin saw was an orang-utan named Jenny at London Zoo in 1838. He was immediately struck by the similarities between her behaviour and that of humans.

• Before Darwin's ideas were published, most people believed that species were unchanging. Concern about extinction was unheard of.

• British naturalist, Alfred Russel Wallace, independently conceived a theory of natural selection identical to Darwin's, based on completely different observations on the other side of the world. Darwin's and Wallace's theories were both presented on the same day in 1858 to the Linnean Society of London.

• 'Survival of the fittest' was not a phrase coined by Darwin. He borrowed it from the economist Herbert Spencer, on Wallace's advice. It does not appear until the fifth edition of Origin of Species.

• Despite being best known for his contribution to biology, Darwin's first scientific paper was on geology.

• The concept of evolution existed before Darwin. However, he was the first person to explain it through natural selection.

Great holiday ideas, offers and competitions. Signup for our free newsletter

FIND OUT ABOUT ALL KINDS OF WATERSPORTS

Before you read

1 Vocabulary

Use a dictionary to help you to match the words in the box to pictures A-E.

ash fireworks jewels diamonds pearls

A ______ B ______ C ______ D ______ E ______

2 Here are some other words. Use a dictionary to discover the meaning.

an emerald a ruby a sapphire a bracelet a locket a necklace

3 How much do you know?

Before you read, see if you can answer these questions. Then check your answers in Chapter Four.

A What do English people like eating? Can you complete 1-3?

1 Fish and ....

2 Stilton ....

3 Roast meat and roast ....

B What do you know about English sport? Can you match the competitions (1-3) to the sports (A-C)

1 ☐	Wimbledon	A football
2 ☐	Test matches	B cricket
3 ☐	The FA Cup	C tennis

England

England is the country in the British Isles with the largest population (over 50 million) and contains the capital of the United Kingdom, London.

What do the English like doing?

track 06

Popular hobbies include gardening and DIY. This means 'do-it-yourself' and it involves repairing or decorating your home. Fishing in rivers is a common activity, especially for men. Teenagers enjoy clubbing – going to nightclubs with their friends. In the past, people went for seaside holidays in places like Brighton, on the south coast, or Scarborough, which is about 70km from York. but now they prefer foreign holidays because it is often cheaper to go abroad. And, of course, shopping is always a popular activity.

Brighton Pier.

What is there to eat in England?

Most English people eat breakfast, lunch (which some families call 'dinner'!) and dinner (which some families call 'tea'). In addition, there are elevenses (a snack at about 11 a.m.), tea (in the afternoon at about 4 p.m.) and supper (a light meal before bed). English food does not have a good reputation [1] in other countries but there are in fact some delicious dishes:

Fish and chips is made using white fish such as cod, haddock or plaice, which is fried in batter. Traditionally, it is eaten with mushy peas, a kind of purée made from green peas.

Roast diner is the traditional English Sunday lunch of roast meat, such as lamb or beef, together with roast potatoes and lots of vegetables. On Christmas Day, most families eat **roast turkey**.

Stilton cheese is a blue cheese with a very strong taste and many people call it the 'King of Cheeses'. But if you prefer other kinds, there are many local varieties of cheese in England, especially in the south-west.

English **cakes** and **biscuits** are very popular with English people and with tourists. A **cream tea** is usually eaten in the afternoon and may include scones,[2] butter, jam and cream. It is typical of Devon and Cornwall in the south-west of England.

1. **reputation** : the opinion of other people about someone or something.
2. **scones** : a type of small cake which you cut in half and fill with butter and/or jam and cream.

A **full English breakfast** is a good way to start the day if you're not on a diet! A traditional breakfast includes sausages, grilled tomatoes, mushrooms, fried eggs, fried bread and a cup of strong **tea.**

Curry is not originally English but the English love curries. Curry came to England from South Asia in the 18th century, but it became very popular after World War II. Today the English's favourite type, Vindaloo, is more popular in the UK than in India!

Sport

The main sporting events in an English year are: the FA Cup [3] (football), the Oxford-Cambridge boat race (rowing), the Grand National and the Derby (horse-racing), Wimbledon (tennis), the Open Golf, the Six Nations (rugby) and international Test Matches (cricket).

The English say that they invented football but so do other countries. However, it has been played since the eighth century. It was so popular in the Middle Ages that some kings banned it

3. **FA Cup**: an important football competition between English (and some Welsh) teams.

University Boat Race.

Cricket match.

because the players became very angry and noisy and it stopped men from preparing for war! The first international football match was between England and Scotland in 1870.

Teams at the top of the English Premier football league are very rich and have some of the best players in the world. The 'Big Four' teams are Manchester United, Chelsea, Arsenal and Liverpool but other teams with rich owners may soon join them.

Cricket is played by many English-speaking nations. In 1882, the Australians beat the English for the first time. The English were so upset that the newspapers said that English cricket was dead and was cremated. [4] Since then, the matches between Australia and England have been called 'the Ashes'. Cricket matches can last for five days, four days or one day. The shortest form of the sport is called 20-20 and England won the world championship in 2010 when they beat strong teams from South Africa, Sri Lanka and Australia.

Celebrations

Christmas and Easter are the most important festivals for the English but there are many others. Most English children look forward to **Fireworks' Night** or Guy Fawkes Night on 5th November. This is to remember that Guy Fawkes did not succeed in killing the King in 1605 (see Chapter 3), but nowadays it is a family festival for

4. **cremated** : burnt; we use this word when the bodies of dead people are burnt.

children. There are fires, fireworks and lots of hot food. In the town of Lewes in Sussex it is a big event and the local people burn huge figures of unpopular politicians and celebrities.

Another date is 1st April or **April Fool's Day**. On this day, people are allowed to play jokes on other people. Even the newspapers and the television take part, like in the 1950s when the BBC showed a programme about spaghetti growing on trees. Some people believed it was true!

Cliffe Bonfire Society members.

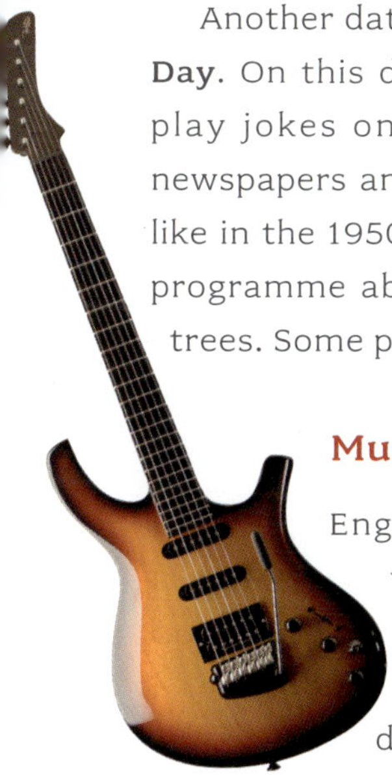

Music

English pop and rock music is popular all over the world. From the Rolling Stones and the Beatles in the 1960s to Elton John to punk[5] bands to Coldplay and Radiohead in the 2000s, it has developed over the years and is still developing now.

Iconic[6] Places

There are many of these, so we will choose only a few. In Chapter Two, you read about **Stonehenge** and **Hadrian's Wall** from the early history of Britain. When the Normans came, they built many castles but the most famous is the **Tower of London**. The White Tower, which you can see from the river Thames, was the original main building. Many people were executed in the Tower, including three queens of England.

5. **punk** : a style of music, clothes and behaviour which developed in the 1970s and 1980s.
6. **iconic** : famous and important. For example, Big Ben is iconic.

Raven Master at the Tower of London.

The Crown Jewels are kept in the Jewel House at the tower. Tourists can see the crown with over 3,000 diamonds and pearls in it. Large black birds called ravens have lived in the Tower since the late eighteenth century. Legend [7] says that if they leave the Tower, something terrible will happen to England, so the government pays for at least six ravens to be there. In fact some feather are cut from their wings so they can't fly away.

As well as castles, England also has many famous cathedrals. **Canterbury Cathedral**, **York Minster, Salisbury and Lincoln Cathedrals** are some of the most beautiful. Members of the royal family get married in **Westminster Abbey** and **St Paul's** in London. There are also many great houses in England such as **Chatsworth House** and **Blenheim Palace**.

British cities which are famous for their beauty include Canterbury, Bath, York, Stratford-on-Avon, Oxford and Cambridge. **Liverpool**, however, is a port city which is also world-

7. **legend** : an old or traditional story which is probably not true but which is well-known.

Liverpool city.

famous. Liverpool is a UNESCO World Heritage site and was a European Capital of Culture in 2008. Liverpool people speak with a strong local accent and have a reputation for being warm, creative and strong. You can visit the Cavern club, where the Beatles started their career, or Anfield, where Liverpool Football Club play. Birmingham, Leeds, Sheffield, Manchester and Bristol are other big cities.

The Lake District is one of the most attractive landscapes in the United Kingdom and was loved by the Romantic poets. It is in the north-west and includes 12 of the largest lakes in England with more than 3,500 kilometres of paths for walkers and cyclists.

England is not famous for its beaches. But if you go to **Newquay** in Cornwall, you can enjoy surfing on the Atlantic coast in the 'Surfing Capital of Great Britain'. The **white cliffs of Dover** are well-known as they are the first thing that you see if you come to England by ship from France. There are many other beautiful pieces of coast.

White cliffs of Dover.

Iconic People

England, like all nations, had many famous people, such as Queen Elizabeth I, Shakespeare, Isaac Newton, Dickens, Darwin and Winston Churchill. Now read about some recent 'iconic people'.

Princess Diana was the wife of Prince Charles but became unhappy in her marriage. Many people all over the worlds loved her for her beauty and her kindness to people with problems, such as AIDS victims. She died in a car crash in Paris in 1997.

John Lennon wrote most of the songs of the Beatles with Paul McCartney. Later, he married Yoko Ono, a Japanese artist, and protested against war. He was murdered in New York in 1980.

Margaret Thatcher was the first woman to become Prime Minister of the UK. She was called the Iron Lady because of her strong ideas on Government. Some British people supported Margaret Thatcher and her ideas but she also had strong enemies.

David Beckham: he is probably the most famous English footballer of the 1990s and 2000s. He played in three World Cups and was England captain. He married one of the Spice Girls, a pop group, and is often in the celebrity pages of magazines and newspapers.

David Beckham.

England is a country with castles, cathedrals and strong traditions; but it is also a place of surprises and new ideas. What is the future? By the end of the 21st century, will there be a royal family? Will Scotland and Wales be independent countries? What will be England's relationship with the rest of Europe? What will be the effect of global warming on the English countryside? Nobody knows the answers.

The text and **beyond**

1 Comprehension check

Complete this fact file about England. Write a word or words in each space. Use information from Chapter Four.

Popular hobbies: Gardening, DIY and **(1)** .... in rivers

Food: Traditional Sunday lunch: roast **(2)** .... and vegetables

Other famous dishes: **(3)** .... and chips; **(4)** ...., originally from India.

Sport: Many famous events, including **(5)** .... (tennis) and the Oxford and Cambridge **(6)** .... on the Thames.

Celebrations: These include: Christmas, Easter and, in November, **(7)** .... Night.

Music: English **(8)** .... and **(9)** .... music is world-famous.

Places: For example, the **(10)** .... of London and many famous **(11)** .... in cities like Canterbury and York. A place of great natural beauty is the **(12)** .... District.

People: For example, **(13)** ...., who died in a car crash.
John **(14)** ...., a member of the Beatles.
Margaret Thatcher, the first female **(15)** .... of the UK.
David Beckham, a **(16)** ...., who has played in Britain, Italy and the USA.

T: GRADE 4

2 Speaking – hobbies and sports

Look again at the first sections in Chapter Four. Then prepare a short talk with similar information about popular activities and hobbies in your country.

You should talk about these four areas:

1 popular hobbies and activities
2 food
3 sport
4 an example of a famous city

PET 3 Notices

Here are some notices that you might see in England. Look at the text in each question. What does it say? Choose the letter next to the correct explanation – A, B or C.

1

A ☐ The fish is caught at night.
B ☐ The fish comes from the area.
C ☐ The café serves fish and chips and also local fish.

2

A ☐ Some spectators pay less than others.
B ☐ The match is played under water.
C ☐ All adults pay £18.

3

A ☐ The display will take place this weekend.
B ☐ The display may take place this weekend.
C ☐ There is bad weather but the display will take place.

4

A ☐ Do not go inside the cathedral now.
B ☐ Please behave well inside the cathedral.
C ☐ It is forbidden to listen to music in the cathedral.

Before you read

1 Vocabulary

Complete the sentences with these people from Chapter Five.

An ancestor   An astronaut   A descendant   A highlander*   A lowlander*   A philosopher   A spectator

1 .... asks 'big' questions about life and about our knowledge and experience.
2 .... may travel to the moon or to Mars.
3 .... is someone in our family in the past, for example your great grandfather.
4 .... lives in the mountains or the hills.
5 .... watches sport or other exciting events.
6 .... is the opposite of '4' and lives on flat land.
7 .... is the opposite of '3', for example your granddaughter.

* We especially use these words for people in Scotland.

2 Listening

track 07

Listen to the first part of Chapter Five twice and complete the advertisement for a book by writing a word or number in each gap.

How long is the cloth that makes a kilt? (**1**) .... metres.
How many different tartans are there? (**2**) ....
When did the (**3**) .... government ban kilts?
(**4**) ....
Why did it ban them? Because they were a symbol of Scottish (**5**) ....
Where did Alan Bean wear a kilt? On the (**6**) ....
Read this book and find the fascinating answers to many more questions.

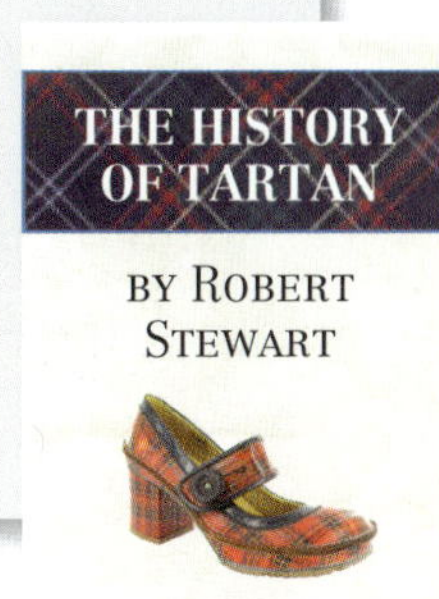

CHAPTER FIVE

Scotland

Scotland has a long, proud history and many national heroes.

Scotland is a land of mountains and lakes with a population of about five million. The Scottish people say some things which you won't hear from English people: these include: 'bairn' for 'child', 'och aye' for 'ah yes' and 'bonny' for 'beautiful'. Let's look at the Scottish culture.

track 07

'Men in Skirts'

The **kilt** is a piece of clothing which many Scottish men wear on special occasions. It consists of one 3-metre piece of cloth which is folded round the body to form the kilt. Traditionally, men wear a sporran with a kilt; it is a kind of large purse that hangs from a belt.

Tartan is the name of the typical coloured pattern;

different tartans are connected with different Scottish families or clans such as the Stewart tartan and the Macdonald tartan. There are more than 4,000 different tartans! In 1746, the English government banned kilts because they thought tartan was a symbol of Scottish independence. Later, in 1969, when Alan Bean, a Scottish-American astronaut on Apollo 12, stood on the moon, he wore tartan.

end

Pipers — the men who play the traditional Scottish musical instrument, the **bagpipes** — usually wear kilts and sporrans.

Food

The most famous Scottish food is **haggis**. This consists of a sheep's stomach which is packed with bits of meat, onion, oats,[1] spices and salt. Robert Burns (see below) wrote about how good haggis is in a famous poem. **Porridge** is another typical Scottish dish. It is made by boiling oats in milk or water and in a traditional Scottish breakfast it is served with salt.

You may prefer Scottish **shortbread**, a delicious butter biscuit. Scotland is also well-known for its very good **Aberdeen Angus beef** and **salmon**.[2]

Iconic Places

Edinburgh is the capital of Scotland and is very popular with tourists, who come to see the Castle and the famous streets such as Princes Street and the Royal Mile. Every August, the Edinburgh Festival takes place. It is one of the most important festivals of theatre and music in the world. Many famous writers

1. **oats** : a cereal.
2. **salmon** : a type of fish.

The city of Edinburgh.

and philosophers have lived in Edinburgh: Robert Louis Stevenson grew up in Edinburgh, and today J. K. Rowling, who wrote 'Harry Potter', lives there.

The **Scottish Highlands** are the mountains and valleys in the northern half of the country. The landscape is magnificent. **Loch Lomond** is the largest lake in Scotland and **Loch Ness** is the most famous (see below). The tallest mountain in the British Isles, **Ben Nevis** (1,343 m), is in the Highlands. People have sometimes taken strange objects to the top of Ben Nevis for fun; a piano and a bed are two examples!

The Highlands have a long, often sad history; many highlanders moved to America or other countries to escape from a difficult and unfair life of poverty. Only about 250,000 people live there now.

Glasgow and **Aberdeen** are other Scottish cities. Aberdeen is the centre of the North Sea oil industry. Aberdeen is so far north that it has less than seven hours daylight in winter and eighteen hours in summer. Glasgow is the largest city in Scotland. In recent years, Franz Ferdinand and Snow Patrol have been successful music bands from the city.

Iconic creatures

The **Loch Ness Monster** is the most famous inhabitant of Scotland! There is a legend that Saint Columba saw a 'water-beast' in the sixth century near Loch Ness. Other witnesses also talked about the monster and there are photographs of what *might* be a huge creature in the lake. Loch Ness is about 250 metres deep, so it is impossible to be absolutely sure whether the monster does or does not exist. Do you believe in Nessie? She is certainly good for the Scottish tourist industry!

Dolly the sheep is another famous Scottish animal. She was cloned [3] at a scientific institute near Edinburgh in 1996; it was the first time that a mammal [4] was cloned.

Iconic People

William Wallace and **Robert the Bruce** were two great Scottish heroes who fought for independence from England in the Middle Ages. Wallace (1272-1305) won a great victory against the English army at Stirling Bridge in 1297, but in the next battle he was defeated. He hid from the English for seven years but was finally arrested and executed. His head was shown to the people on London Bridge.

3. **cloned** : copied, using a scientific process.
4. **mammal** : an animal such as a dog, elephant or a person.

Every Scottish person knows the story of Robert the Bruce (1274-1329) and the spider. He was put in prison by the English. He said that when he was in prison, he watched a spider trying six times to make a web. The spider finally succeeded the seventh time. This example taught him to keep trying. Bruce escaped from prison and defeated King Edward II's English army at the famous Battle of Bannockburn in 1314. He was King of Scotland from 1306 to 1329.

Mary Queen of Scots had a dramatic and very sad life. She was crowned Queen of Scots when she was a baby in 1543.

- She married a French prince when she was only fifteen and lived in France.
- After his death, she returned as Queen to Scotland.
- She was a Catholic, so Protestant Scots hated her.
- Her male secretary, Rizzio, was murdered by her husband in front of her. Was Rizzio her lover?
- Her second husband was murdered. Did Mary arrange this?
- She married for a third time but she had to run away from Scotland.
- She was in prison in England for nearly twenty years.
- She planned to take the place of her cousin, Elizabeth I, as Queen of England.
- She was beheaded in Fotheringhay Castle in Northamptonshire in 1587.
- Her son James later became King of England.

Mary Stuart, Queen of Scots, Nicholas Hilliard.

Robert Burns is Scotland's national poet. As a young man, he worked on his family farm but his poems in the Scottish dialect became very popular. He died when he was only thirty-seven but his poems live on. He wrote the words of 'Auld Lang Syne', which means 'long long ago' and is the song that people sing at New Year. Another famous poem begins 'My luve (love) is like a red, red rose'.

There are many other famous Scottish people. There are writers like **Sir Walter Scott**, **Robert Louis Stevenson** and **Sir Arthur Conan Doyle**, who created Sherlock Holmes. There are actors like **Sean Connery**, who played James Bond. There are singers like **Susan Boyle**, who was in the *Britain's Got Talent* competition in 2009 and became internationally famous. There are many famous scientists and inventors, for example **James Watt**, who invented the steam engine, **Alexander Bell**, who invented the telephone, **Alexander Fleming**, who discovered penicillin, [5] and **John Logie Baird**, who invented television.

5. **penicillin** : an antibiotic (medicine) which has prevented many serious diseases.

Alexander Fleming (1881-1955).

Sport

Glasgow has the two best-known Scottish football teams, Rangers and Celtic. When they play against each other, it is a special occasion. Sir Alex Ferguson, the most successful manager of Manchester United, is Scottish. Golf is another popular sport, while in the winter you can go skiing in the Highlands.

The Highland Games is a typical Scottish sporting event. It is like a Scottish Olympics. The events include 'tossing the caber', when men have to throw a long piece of tree trunk. You have to be very strong and very skilled to win this competition! You can see Highland Games all over North America but one of the most important ones is held every year in California, with more than 50,000 spectators.

The caber toss, a traditional Scottish athletic event.

Celebrations

New Year is more important than Christmas in Scotland. The Scottish have a special celebration on 31st December known as '**Hogmanay**'. There are street parties in Edinburgh and Glasgow and other cities. In Stonehaven, there is 'fireball swinging'. All over Scotland and in other countries where Scottish people live Hogmanay is celebrated and 'Auld Lang Syne' is sung.

The Stonehaven Hogmanay Fireball Celebrations.

Burns Night takes place on the birthday of Robert Burns, 25th January. People read poems and sing songs by Burns. The centre of a traditional Burns Night is a haggis. A piper plays as the haggis is carried into the room and, before it is cut, someone reads Burns's poem 'To a Haggis'. Like Hogmanay, Burns Night is celebrated not only in Scotland but by people in many countries who have Scottish ancestors.

Let's close this chapter on Scotland with a part of a song by Robert Burns. It says that men all over the world shall be brothers:

It's coming yet for a' that,
That Man to Man, the world o'er,
Shall brothers be for a' that.

The text and **beyond**

PET

1 Comprehension check

Decide if each sentence (1-8) is correct or incorrect. If it is correct, mark A. If it is not correct, mark B.

		A	B
1	English people don't normally use words such as 'bairn' for 'child'.	☐	☐
2	It is forbidden to wear tartan now.	☐	☐
3	Visitors can play the piano on top of Ben Nevis.	☐	☐
4	Everyone is now certain that the Loch Ness Monster does not exist.	☐	☐
5	Robert Bruce learnt something important by watching a spider.	☐	☐
6	Mary was Queen of France, then Queen of Scotland and then Queen of England.	☐	☐
7	In the Highland Games, mountain climbing is one of the main activities.	☐	☐
8	Hogmanay is the Scottish New Year celebration.	☐	☐

2 Vocabulary

How many words with a Scottish connection can you find in this wordsearch? The words may be horizontal, vertical or diagonal.

M	O	U	N	T	A	I	N
B	X	S	O	A	G	R	E
A	Z	P	I	R	O	E	W
G	K	I	L	T	L	T	Y
P	U	D	W	A	F	S	E
I	C	E	W	N	S	B	A
P	G	R	Z	T	E	O	R
E	G	X	A	W	Q	M	B
S	P	O	R	R	A	N	Z

PET 3 Reading

Read the section Iconic People on pages 61-63. For each question, choose the correct letter — A, B, C or D.

1 What does the writer say about Robert the Bruce?

A ☐ He was a friend of William Wallace.
B ☐ He wanted Scotland to be independent.
C ☐ He had a pet spider when he was in prison.
D ☐ The story about the spider isn't true.

2 What do we learn about Mary Queen of Scots from the text?

A ☐ Her life was full of problems.
B ☐ She enjoyed marriage.
C ☐ She murdered one of her husbands.
D ☐ She was very religious.

3 Why does the writer include Robert Burns in this section?

A ☐ because he wrote in the Scottish dialect
B ☐ because he was a farmer
C ☐ because his songs and poems are very popular in Scotland
D ☐ because he died when he was still young

4 Which of these does the text tell us?

A ☐ Scottish people are different from the English.
B ☐ Scotland has produced famous writers and scientists.
C ☐ Scotland has had many kings and queens.
D ☐ The Scottish know a lot about their own history.

PET 4 Writing

This is part of a letter you receive from your friend Sarah.

> My Dad's got a job in Scotland, so we are going to live there for a year. I don't know anything about the life there. I know that you've read about Scotland. Can you tell me anything?

Now write a letter to Sarah. Use information from Chapter Five or from the Internet. Write your letter in about 100 words.

The British Isles and Films

There are thousands of films that take place in the British Isles. Here are some that are about England, Scotland, Wales and Northern and Southern Ireland.

Films about English Queens

In 1998, Cate Blanchett starred as Queen Elizabeth I in the film ***Elizabeth***. The film starts when the Catholic Queen Mary is in power. The young Elizabeth is in danger as she is a Protestant and has many enemies. When Mary dies, the new queen's supporters want her to get married so that she can have a son who will be king after her. But Elizabeth doesn't get married and she doesn't have any children. For her part in the film, Cate Blanchett won a British Academy Award [1] and a Golden Globe Award for Best Actress and several other awards. A second film, ***Elizabeth, the Golden Age*** (2007), was not so successful although it won an Oscar for its costumes.

In 2009, the slogan for a film about the early years of Queen Victoria said 'Love rules all'. This was ***The Young Victoria*** with Emily Blunt playing the eighteen-year-old queen. The film shows the love which grows between Victoria and Albert. It won several awards, including an Oscar for its costumes.

The Queen was a 2006 film about Queen Elizabeth II at the time that Princess Diana died. The role of the Queen was played by Helen

1. **awards** : prize.

Mirren, who won an Oscar in 2007 for her performance. Other actors played real-life characters, such as Prince Charles, the Prime Minister Tony Blair and his wife Cherie.

Braveheart, a Scottish warrior

The American actor Mel Gibson both directed and acted the hero in the film ***Braveheart***. The film is about the life of William Wallace (see Chapter 5). Although, it is not historically accurate, it is a good adventure story. After the woman who Wallace loves is killed, he fights against the English king Edward I. Princess Isabelle of France falls in love with Wallace and helps him to escape from danger but finally he is put in prison. The film ends with his death as he cries 'Freedom!' for Scotland. The film won five Oscars in 1996, including one for 'best picture'.

Mel Gibson in *Braveheart*, 1995.

Dancing at Lughnasa, 1998.

An Irish story

Meryl Streep starred in ***Dancing at Lughnasa***, a 1998 film about five unmarried sisters who live in the country in Ireland in the 1930s. Lughnasa is an ancient summer pre-Christian [2] festival when rules are broken. There is disagreement between Christian religion and ancient Celtic religion in the film. The women are limited by the strong religious rules of Ireland in the 1930s but they also want love and freedom. But they cannot get their dreams. Although the story of the film is sad, there are lots of funny moments. Meryl Streep is a famous American actress who has won two Oscars in her career and many other awards. She has an Irish great-grandmother and after she made this film, she wanted to spend more time in Ireland.

2. **pre-Christian** : before the time of Christianity.

Kings and Mountains in Wales

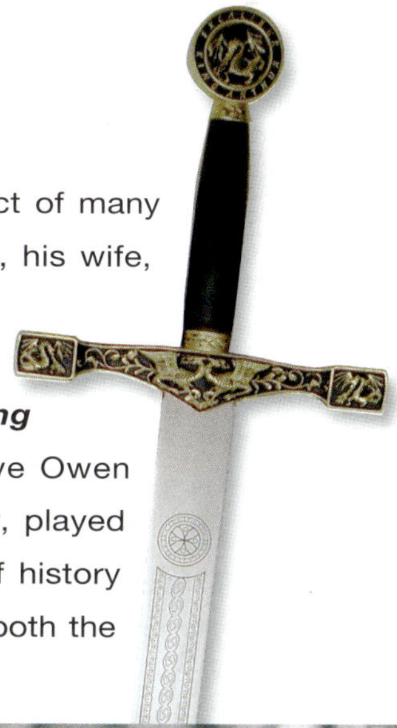

King Arthur (see Chapter 7) has been the subject of many films. The love affair between Queen Guinevere, his wife, and Lancelot, one of his knights, has been the subject of most of these films, such as *Camelot* (1967) and *Excalibur* (1981). In the 2004 film ***King Arthur***, Keira Knightley played Guinevere, Clive Owen played Arthur and Ioann Gruffud, a Welsh actor, played Lancelot. The film places Arthur in the period of history after the Romans left Britain and he has to fight both the Anglo-Saxons and the Britons.

King Arthur, 2004.

Oscar-winner Hugh Grant starred in a film called ***The Englishman Who Went Up a Hill But Came Down a Mountain*** (1995). What a strange title! The people in a Welsh village are angry when an arrogant man from London tells them that their local 'mountain' is not tall enough to be a real mountain and must be named a 'hill' on the map. Finally, the villagers add rocks to the top of the hill and it becomes a 'mountain'. The film is a comedy and tells us a lot about the relationships between the Welsh and the English.

1 Comprehension check

There are 20 mistakes in this fact-file about the films. Can you find the mistakes and correct them?

TITLE	DATE	MAIN ACTOR(S)	OTHER INFORMATION
The Englishman Who Went Up a Mountain But Came Down a Hill	1995	Hugh Grantley	Some Irish people are angry when a man from London comes to their village.
Braveheart	1996	William Wallace	It is directed by the main actor.
Elizabeth II	1998	Cate Blanchett	Cate Blanchett won an Oscar for this film.
Dancing at Easter	2006	Meryl Streep	Meryl Streep is an Irish actress. She has never won an Oscar.
King Arthur	1967	Keira Knightley and Lancelot	Keira Knightley won an Oscar for this film.
The Queen of England	2007	Helen Mirren and Prince Charles	Helen Mirren won an Oscar for this film.
Love Rules All	2009	Emilia Blunt	A film about Queen Victoria when she was old.

INTERNET PROJECT

Richard the Third

Connect to the Internet and go to www.blackcat-cideb.com. Insert the title or part of the title of the book into our search engine. Open the page for *The British Isles*. Click on the internet project link. Then answers the following questions.

Richard the Third is a play by Shakespeare; there is a famous film of the play starring Laurence Olivier. It is an old black-and-white film but it is still enjoyable. King Richard III was a real person in the history of England. Some people think that he murdered two young princes because he wanted to be king.

1 What were the names of the Princes?
2 Where did King Richard put them?
3 How old were the princes?
4 What did people find in 1674?
5 Does the new research say that the princes were murdered?
6 According to the new research, who was with Richard at the Battle of Bosworth?
7 Who won the Battle of Bosworth?
8 Which queen was held later in the same place as the Princes? For how long?
9 Who has written a new book about the Princes?

6 ACTIVITIES

Before you read

1 Vocabulary

Use a dictionary to help you match the people in the box with the definitions.

commissioner giant monk outlaw pirate rock or pop star

1 this person is usually on a ship and robs other ships ....
2 this person may work in an office and is very important ....
3 this person is famous because s/he plays music, especially for young people ....
4 this man lives away from other people for religious reasons ....
5 this person lives outside normal society, e.g. Robin Hood in the forest ....
6 you often read about this very tall person in stories for young children ....

2 How much do you know?

How much do you already know about Ireland? Choose the correct word/phrase in each sentence. Now read Chapter Six up to the end of The Economy and check your answers.

1 The national colour of Ireland is *red/blue/green*.
2 Irish stew contains *lamb/beef/cream*.
3 An average Irish person drinks *100/6/12* cups of tea every day.
4 Hurling is a *sport/dance/festival*.
5 On 26th December, many Irish people *visit their grandparents/have a special Christmas meal/go to the horse races*.
6 Which of these music groups are Irish? *The Rolling Stones/U2/Coldplay*.
7 Danny Boy is *an Irish hero/a song/a racehorse*.
8 People called Ireland *The Celtic Tiger/The Green Lion/Riverdance*.

CHAPTER **SIX**

Ireland

The national colour of Ireland is green, and it is certainly a very green and beautiful island, with a lot of farms, lakes, hills and mountains.

Food

track 08

You can eat well in Ireland; there is fresh fish and seafood from the lakes and the ocean, and fresh meat and vegetables from the farms. The national dish, **Irish stew**, is made from lamb, potatoes, onions, carrots and parsley. The Irish are even more fond of drinking **tea** than the English, and an average Irish person drinks six cups a day.

Sport

The national sport of Ireland is **Gaelic football**. It differs from normal football in many ways: there are fifteen players in each team; the goals are H-shaped; you can hit the ball with your hand as well as kicking it. Another Irish sport is **hurling**. In this sport, you hit the ball with a stick.

What do you do in Ireland on 26th December, the day after Christmas? You go to the horse races. Horse racing has a long history in Ireland and many of the world's best horses, riders and trainers have been Irish. Other popular sports are rugby, football and golf.

Music and Dance

In many countries traditional music has died out, but not in Ireland. The love for typical Irish music is still very strong. Irish dancing is also popular and the show Riverdance was an international success. There are also many Irish rock and pop stars. Have you heard of U2 (they have sold over 170 million CDs), Boyzone, Westlife, Enya or Van Morrison?

The best-known traditional Irish song is probably 'Danny Boy' – but although the music is Irish, the words were written by an Englishman! You can listen to it on the Internet. The song is about someone who is sad because 'Danny boy' must leave; is he going to fight in a war or is he leaving to find work? The song doesn't tell us.

Riverdance Premiere in Berlin.

The Economy [1]

Ireland has been a poor country with many problems but from 1995 to 2007 there was an economic boom there. This means that the Irish economy grew fast. Lots of new houses were built, new companies grew, there were more jobs in Ireland and lots of people from the new European countries moved there. People called Ireland the 'Celtic Tiger' at this time. Unfortunately, as in many other countries, the Irish economy got worse after 2008.

Iconic places

Dublin is the capital of the Republic of Ireland. It is a beautiful city with Georgian buildings, a castle, art galleries and a famous theatre, the Abbey Theatre. The River Liffey passes through the centre of Dublin, and there are many famous bridges such as O'Connell Bridge, Ha'penny Bridge and the modern Millenium Bridge. In 1916 there was The Easter Rising in Dublin. This was a part of the revolution by Irish Republicans against the English. Some of the Republicans organised the revolution from inside the **Post Office** and you can still see the bullet [2] holes in the stone.

1. **Economy** : the financial condition of a country.
2. **bullet** : the thing that a gun shoots.

Ha'penny bridge, Dublin.

Trinity College, Dublin, is the most important Irish university, like Oxford or Cambridge in England. In the library you can see the **Book of Kells**, a beautiful book that is more than 1,200 years old. The book contains parts of the Bible. The detailed pictures were painted by Irish monks.

Belfast is the capital of Northern Ireland. For many years it was divided between the Catholics and the Protestants. There was a lot of fighting but since the Good Friday Agreement was signed in 1998 (see Chapter 3), it has been peaceful.

The Giant's Causeway is on the east coast of Northern Ireland. It was formed naturally 50-60 million years ago by a volcano. [3] There are about 40,000 columns of rock which look like a man-made road. There is a legend which says that an Irish giant made this type of bridge by throwing rocks in the sea so that he could cross to Scotland to fight a Scottish giant.

Giant's Causeway in Northern Ireland.

In the walls of **Blarney castle** near the city of Cork is an ancient piece of bluestone called **the Blarney Stone**. People believe that if you kiss the stone you will start to speak very well. But to reach the stone you have to hang down from the top of the castle wall and put your life in danger! Nowadays, there are rails to keep you safe and many tourists come to 'kiss the Blarney Stone'.

3. **volcano** : 

The west coast of Ireland on the Atlantic Ocean is famous for its great beauty. In the south-west of Ireland, the **Lakes of Killarney** are in a ring of mountains. The lakes are a good place to eat the local fish, called trout.

In many places there are very tall **round towers.** The most famous ones are at the **Rock of Cashel** and at **Glendalough**. They were built in the Middle Ages and the tallest is forty metres high.

Iconic People

There are many Irish heroes. Did you know that some Presidents of the USA had Irish ancestors — for example, **Teddy Roosevelt**, **J F Kennedy**, **Ronald Reagan** and **Bill Clinton**? Even **Barack Obama**'s mother's family came from Ireland. The famous outlaw, **Billy the Kid**, was Irish too! There are many famous Irish writers and artists, for example **G. B. Shaw**, **W. B. Yeats**, **Samuel Beckett** and **Seamus Heaney**, who all won the Nobel prize. **Oscar Wilde** was also Irish. Here are some examples of recent Irish iconic people:

If you ask the question 'Who was the greatest footballer in the world?' in Northern Ireland, there is only one answer, '**George Best**'. If you don't believe this, look at videos of his play on the Internet. He played for Manchester United and of course, Northern Ireland.

Bob Geldof was the leader of an Irish punk band, the Boomtown Rats, but soon became famous for his fight against world poverty. He formed Band Aid to raise money for Ethiopia in 1984 and organised Live Aid, a rock concert, in 1985. He is still active and tries to help poor nations.

The round tower of Glendalough.

Mary Robinson was the first woman president of Ireland between 1990 and 1997, and was later the United Nations High Commissioner for Human Rights.[4] She has fought for the rights of women and has also done a lot for the poor and hungry. In 2009, she received the Presidential Medal of Freedom from the U.S. President Barack Obama. She has worked with Nelson Mandela and other world politicians.

Saint Patrick

Who was Saint Patrick?
He wasn't Irish (maybe he was Welsh or Scottish) but Irish pirates caught him.

- He was a slave in Ireland.
- He escaped, but returned to Ireland around CE 450.
- He converted the Irish people to Christianity.

A legend says that Saint Patrick drove all the snakes out of Ireland and today there are no wild snakes there.

The Irish celebrate St Patrick's Day on 17th March with special parades. These take place not just in Ireland but anywhere where there are Irish communities. For example, in 2010, Sydney Opera House in Australia was turned green by special lights. In New York, about 250,000 people take part in the parade on Fifth Avenue.

4. **Human Rights** : the idea of freedom for every person.

Sydney Opera House.

Stories from the past

There are lots of stories in Ireland about leprechauns or 'the little people'. Leprechauns are little old men who wear green or red jackets, carry a stick and wear a tall hat. If you catch a leprechaun, maybe you will find his pot of gold and he might give you three wishes. But they enjoy playing tricks and you shouldn't trust them. Many Irish people don't like this image of leprechauns, which they think is something just to please the tourists.

There are many Celtic legends. One of these is about 'Deirdre of the Sorrows'.[5] Deirdre was a beautiful young woman but when she was a baby, the druids (see Chapter Two) said that she would cause the death of many men. The King sent her to live in the forest until she was a teenager. Then he wanted to marry her. But Deirdre fell in love with another man and married him, and then they escaped to Scotland. After seven years, the King said that he forgave them, so they returned to Ireland. But the king had lied. Deirdre's husband and his brothers were killed and Deirdre died of a broken heart.

Ireland has not had an easy history. For centuries, the English controlled the country. It is divided into the Republic of Ireland and Northern Ireland; there has been a difficult division between Roman Catholics and Protestants. It has experienced the Potato Famine, the War of Independence and the 'troubles' (see Chapter 3). In the past many Irish people went to live in other countries, because they wanted to escape from poverty. But anyone with Irish blood is proud to be Irish.

5. **Sorrows** : sadness.

The text and **beyond**

1 Comprehension check

Read the summary of Chapter Six below. In each space write one or two words.

Ireland is a green and beautiful land. Its national dish is (1) .... and its national sport is (2) .... Traditional Irish music and dancing is popular; the show (3) .... was successful all over the world. (4) .... is the capital of Northern Ireland and (5) .... is the capital of Eire. There are many interesting places in Ireland; one of these is (6) .... Tourists come here to kiss a special stone. There are many famous Irish people, including (7) .... She was the (8) .... of Eire and also worked for the United Nations. Saint (9) .... is the national saint of Ireland. There are special parades all over the world on 17th (10) .... Ireland has many old stories and legends. Some of these stories are about (11) .... ; these are little men who play tricks on human beings. (12) '........................ of the Sorrows' is another old Irish story.

PET 2

Read the section Iconic Places again. Decide if each statements about famous Irish places is correct or incorrect. If it is correct, mark A. If it is not correct, mark B.

		A	B
1	There are three famous modern bridges in Dublin.	☐	☐
2	Dublin Post Office is connected to the Easter Rising.	☐	☐
3	The Book of Kells is over 1,000 years old.	☐	☐
4	Belfast is the capital of Ireland.	☐	☐
5	The Giant's Causeway was built a long time ago.	☐	☐
6	The west coast is one of the most beautiful areas in Ireland.	☐	☐
7	Trout live in the Lakes of Killarney.	☐	☐
8	There are two very tall round towers in Ireland.	☐	☐

3 Vocabulary – opposites

Give the adjective which has the opposite meaning to the underlined adjective in the sentences. The first one has been done for you.

0 Dublin is a beautiful city. ....ugly.........
1 Horse-racing is popular in Ireland. ....
2 The economy got worse after 2008. ....
3 Kissing the Blarney stone used to be dangerous. ....
4 The tallest tower is forty metres tall. ....
5 Some leprechauns play nasty tricks. ....

4 Passive verbs

Complete the sentences with the verb in brackets in the passive form. Choose Present Simple or Past Simple forms, depending on the sentence. There are two examples.

0 St Patrick's Day ..is celebrated.. on March 17th. (*celebrate*)
00 Deirdre's husband and brothers ...were killed... . (*kill*)
1 Irish stew .... from lamb, potatoes, onions, carrots and parsley. (*make*)
2 The words of 'Danny Boy' .... by an Englishman. (*write*)
3 From 1995 to 2007, lots of new houses .... (*build*)
4 During that period, Ireland .... the 'Celtic Tiger'. (*call*)
5 The pictures in the Book of Kells .... by monks. (*paint*)

T: GRADE 5

5 Speaking – Festivals and music

In Chapter 6, you read about festivals and music in Ireland. Talk about these questions with a partner.

1 Talk about a festival in your country.
2 Do you think traditional festivals will continue to be popular in the future?
3 What types of music do you enjoy listening to?
4 Is music an important part of life in your country?
5 Do you and your parents listen to different types of music?

Before you read

1 What do you know about Wales?

Before you read Chapter Seven, answer these questions to see how much you already know. Then check your answers as you read.

1 Do the children in Wales learn Welsh in school?
2 What is the eldest son of a British king or queen called?
3 Is an Eisteddfod something that you eat or something that you visit?
4 What is Snowdon, a mountain, a city or a lake?

2 Vocabulary

Use a dictionary to help you match the words in the box with pictures.

a choir a cloak seaweed a wolf

A

B

C

D

3 Listening

track 09

Listen to the beginning of Chapter Seven and choose the correct answer – A, B or C.

1 In Wales you will see a lot of
A ☐ sheep. B ☐ trees. C ☐ ships.

2 To prepare Welsh rarebit, you need
A ☐ cheese. B ☐ lamb. C ☐ rabbit.

3 Bara Brith is the Welsh name of a type of
A ☐ fruit. B ☐ fruit juice. C ☐ cake.

4 A popular sport in Wales is
A ☐ snooker. B ☐ tennis. C ☐ swimming.

Wales

Wales is the English name for this country but Cymru is its name in Welsh.

track 09

Wales and England have always had a close relationship. In the 13th century, the English king Edward I and his armies took control of Wales away from Llewellyn ap Gruffud. He was the grandson of Llewellyn the Great (see later in this chapter). When Henry VIII was king, in the period from 1536 to 1543, England and Wales became one country and English laws covered all the area. But the modern Welsh nationalist political party, Plaid Cymru (in English, The Party in Wales), wants independence for Wales. Plaid Cymru often works with the Scottish Nationalist Party, who want independence for Scotland.

Welsh is a living language: about 25 per cent of Welsh people know it well, although they also know English. All children learn Welsh in schools and teachers must know Welsh. There is Welsh language TV and newspapers, and the signs in towns are in Welsh and English.

Wales is an interesting country that has many special customs, beautiful places and important people.

Food

If you visit Wales, you will see a lot of sheep in the countryside. So it's not surprising that Welsh lamb is often on the menu! Your breakfast in Wales may include black laverbread, which is a paste made with the same type of seaweed that the Japanese use to make sushi. Despite its name, it isn't bread. Other typical Welsh dishes are Welsh rarebit (cheese on toast made in a special way) and Bara Brith (Welsh fruit cake).

Sport

Rugby is the most popular sport in Wales and the Stadium called Cardiff Arms Park is the home of Welsh rugby. The Wales team take part in the 'Six Nations' competition, where they play England, Scotland, Ireland, France and Italy. Football, cricket and snooker are also popular. You can also go surfing on many beaches in Wales.

end

The Land of Song

Wales is called the 'land of song', and the Welsh national song is called 'Land of my Fathers'. Wales is famous for its men's choirs and they often sing before rugby matches. When the iron industry and coalfields were important in South Wales, the factory workers and miners[1] often formed choirs. Today industry and coal-mining are less important in Wales but the tradition of singing continues.

Katherine Jenkins and Bryn Terfel are two successful opera singers from Wales. There have also been several successful international singing stars, such as Tom Jones, Shirley Bassey (see page 90) and Duffy, and bands such as the Manic Street Preachers.

The Eisteddfod

Eisteddfod is a Welsh word which means 'to be sitting together'. An Eisteddfod is an annual meeting of poets, musicians, singers and sometimes dancers who compete for prizes. It is an ancient Welsh tradition which started in 1176. The most important Eisteddfod is the National Eisteddfod of Wales; it attracts over 6,000 competitors[2] and more than 150,000 visitors. The Eisteddfods are symbols of the Welsh love of poetry, music and song.

At an Eisteddfod, you may see women in Welsh national dress. This is a tall black hat and a red cloak. There is no special costume for men.

1. **miners** : people who take useful minerals, such as coal, out of the ground.
2. **competitors** : people who take part in a competition.

Three Cliffs Bay.

Iconic places

Cardiff is the capital of Wales and the location of the Millennium Stadium, where rugby and football are played. Cardiff was named European City of Sport in 2009. The second largest city in Wales is **Swansea**. In the past it was a centre of the coal and the copper industry. A famous Welsh poet, Dylan Thomas (1914-1953), was born here.

Near Swansea there are some prize-winning beaches: **Oxwich Bay,** with 5 kilometres of sands, which was named 'the most beautiful beach in Britain'; **Three Cliffs Bay**, which is called 'Britain's best beach'; **Rhossili Bay**, which was called 'the British supermodel [3] of beaches'!

Saint David's is the smallest city in the UK, with under 2,000 people, but it has a magnificent cathedral. In fact, in Europe a town is called a city because it has a cathedral. Saint David, the saint of Wales, is buried in the cathedral in Saint David's.

3. **supermodel** : top fashion model. Here the most beautiful of all beaches.

Snowdonia is a national park in North Wales. It includes mountains, lakes, rivers, waterfalls, forests and coast. The name comes from the highest mountain, Mount **Snowdon** (1,085 metres). You can walk to the top of the mountain or, if you're lazy, take the little red train, the Snowdon Mountain railway. The film *Tomb Raider 2* with Angelina Jolie was filmed in Snowdonia. 'Snowdon' is the English name; the Welsh call it 'Yr Wyddfa'.

The English king Edward I wanted to control Wales, so he built huge **castles** to protect Wales. Today these castles are attractive for tourists, but in the thirteenth century they were a symbol of English power. Four of the most important castles that you can see today are **Caernarfon**, **Harlech**, **Beaumaris** and **Conwy**. Caernarfon castle is connected with the Prince of Wales, the eldest son of the monarch. In 1284, Edward I's son was born here and this is why the first son of a monarch is called the Prince of Wales.

Portmeirion is an Italian-style village in North Wales. Sir Clough Williams-Ellis, who designed the village, said that he wanted to bring the colour and beauty of the Mediterranean to this area of Wales.

There are many other beautiful areas in Wales, such as **Cardigan Bay**, the **Pembrokeshire Coast**, the island of **Anglesey**, and interesting towns like **Aberystwyth**, **Bangor** and **Llandudno**. As for castles, there are more castles in Wales per person than anywhere else in the world.

Caernarfon Castle.

Iconic people

Two heroes of the Welsh people are **Llewellyn the Great** (1173-1240) and **Owen Glendower** (c.f. 1354-1416). In the thirteenth century, Llewellyn kept Wales independent from the Norman kings of England. Glendower was a nationalist leader who led a revolution against the English king, Henry IV, from 1400 to 1412. At first he was successful and in 1404 he created an Independent Welsh Parliament, but in 1405 he was defeated by Henry's son.

There is a legend about Llewellyn's dog, called Gellert. Gellert had to guard the king's baby son while Llewellyn was away. He killed a wolf that tried to attack the child. When Llewellyn returned, he couldn't see the baby and there was blood on the dog's mouth, so he killed the dog. But then he found the baby safe under its bed.

Henry Morgan was a Welsh pirate who robbed ships and towns in the Caribbean in the seventeenth century, a real 'pirate of the Caribbean'. To some people he is a hero, to others he is a criminal of the sea.

In recent times, there have been many famous Welsh people: writers like **Dylan Thomas**; actors like **Catherine Zeta Jones** and **Anthony Hopkins**, who played Hannibal Lecter in *Silence of the Lambs*; politicians like **Aneurin Bevan**, who began the National Health Service in the UK. **Richard Burton** was the first world-famous Welsh actor; he married Elizabeth Taylor and they starred together in *Cleopatra*.

Shirley Bassey grew up in Tiger Bay, which was then the dangerous port area of Cardiff. She has had a long career in show business since she began performing in 1953. She is famous for singing the title songs for three James Bond films: *Goldfinger*, *Diamonds are Forever* and *Moonraker*.

Welsh legends: King Arthur and Branwen

Have you heard the stories of King Arthur and the knights of the round table? Some people say that his castle, Camelot, was in Wales but others say it was in south-west England or Brittany in France. Certainly, the first time that anyone wrote about Arthur was in Welsh literature. Many people think that the real Arthur was a Celt who fought against the Anglo-Saxons.

On Bardsey Island, off the north-west coast of Wales, there is a cave where local stories say that Arthur and Merlin, a wizard [4] who gave advice to Arthur, are buried. Is it true? Was King Arthur Welsh? Did he exist?

Another legend is about a girl called Branwen, whose brother was a giant, and a king in Wales. Branwen married the Irish king but when he took her to Ireland he was very unkind to her. Branwen sent news to her brother by a bird which flew across the sea between Ireland and Wales. Her brother walked through the sea to help his sister. There was a terrible war and many people were killed, including the Welsh and Irish kings. Branwen returned to Wales with the head of her dead brother and was sad about what happened.

Wales is a small country with a population of only about 3 million. But it has its own identity and its own strong Celtic culture.

4. **wizard**: man with magic power.

Welsh coast.

The text and **beyond**

1 Comprehension check

Correct the mistake in each sentence. The first one is an example.

0 50% of people in Wales know Welsh well.
25% of people in Wales know Welsh well ....

1 Black laverbread is a type of Japanese bread.

2 Swansea is the capital of Wales.

3 The national park is called Snowdonia because it snows a lot there.

4 Portmeirion is an Italian village where a lot of Welsh people live.

5 Llewellyn's dog killed his baby son.

6 Richard Burton played Hannibal Lecter in *Silence of the Lambs.*

2 Vocabulary

Wales is the 'Land of Song'. Can you complete the words about music and song below.

1	Someone who plays music.	a mus _ _ _ an
2	A group of people who sing.	a c _ _ _ r
3	You go to this to listen to people sing or play music.	a con _ _ _ t
4	Someone who plays the guitar.	a guitar _ _ _
5	This is music, song and drama.	o _ _ _ _

3 Prepositions

Write a suitable preposition in each of these sentences from Chapter seven. Then check your answers in the chapter.

1 Wales is the English name .... this country.

2 The Wales team take part .... the 'Six Nations' competition.

3 Bryn Terfel is a successful opera singer .... Wales.

4 In 1405 he was defeated .... Henry's son.

5 But then he found the baby safe .... its bed.

6 Perhaps Arthur fought .... the Anglo-Saxons.

7 Merlin gave advice .... Arthur.

PET 4 Reading

Read the text below and choose the correct word for each space.

THE ISLE OF ANGLESEY

Anglesey is an island near the north-west coast of Wales. In the Middle Ages, people called the island 'the Mother of Wales' because the farms provided so **(1)** .... food.
There is an old castle on Anglesey in the town of Beaumaris. **(2)** .... was built by King Edward I after he defeated the Welsh princes. **(3)** .... important town on the island is Holyhead; ferries go **(4)** .... here to Ireland.
There is a famous village in Anglesey. It has the longest name of any place in the United Kingdom. **(5)** .... name is *Llanfairpwllgwyngyllgogerych-wyrndrobwllllantysiliogogogoch**. It was invented **(6)** .... the nineteenth century to attract tourists! Local people call it Llanfairpwll **(7)** .... it is easier to say.

* This name means in English: 'The church of St. Mary in a hollow of white hazel near a rapid whirlpool and near St. Tysilio's church by the red cave'. Use a dictionary to help you to understand this.

1	**A** many	**B** more	**C** very	**D** much
2	**A** He	**B** It's	**C** It	**D** Its
3	**A** Other	**B** Extra	**C** Another	**D** Second
4	**A** from	**B** after	**C** on	**D** between
5	**A** It's	**B** Its	**C** His	**D** Their
6	**A** by	**B** in	**C** on	**D** while
7	**A** during	**B** but	**C** why	**D** because

PET 5 Writing

This is part of a letter you receive from a Welsh friend Owen.

I've told you a lot about the famous places in Wales. When you come to stay with me, which ones would you like to visit?

Now write a letter to Owen in about 100 words.

1 The British Isles Quiz

Answer these questions about the information in this book. You get one point for each correct answer.

Total points:

30-40 You deserve a British or an Irish passport!

25-29 Very good 20-24 Good

Section One: Geography

1 What is the name of the sea on the east coast of Great Britain?
2 What is the tallest mountain in the UK?
3 What natural feature was formed by volcanic action?
4 In which country is the Lake District?
5 Which UK islands are closer to France than to England?
6 In which country is Snowdonia?
7 What is the second largest city in Wales?
8 Where are the Lakes of Killarney?

Section Two: Customs and languages

1 When is Guy Fawkes Night?
2 Where would you see someone tossing the caber?
3 What is Geordie?
4 According to a legend, what did St Patrick remove from Ireland?
5 Which flower is the national symbol of Wales?
6 What is the English translation of 'Shwmae'?
7 What is the national song of Wales?
8 Who celebrates Hogmanay and when?

Section Three: **People**

What is the name of...

1 the last English king who was killed in battle?

2 the English king who had six wives?

3 the man who tried to kill King James I?

4 the first Prime Minister to live at 10 Downing Street?

5 the owner of a dog called Gellert?

6 the Scottish leader who learnt a lesson from a spider?

7 the national saints of England, Wales and Scotland?

8 the first female Irish President?

Section Four: **Places**

Where is...

1 the cathedral where Thomas Becket was killed?

2 the Abbey Theatre?

3 the Scottish Parliament?

4 a stone that people come to kiss?

5 the Tynwald?

6 the Book of Kells?

7 Hadrian's Wall?

8 the 2008 European Capital of Culture?

Section Five: **Countries**

Which country...

1 was called the Celtic Tiger?

2 experienced 'the Troubles'?

3 fought with England during the Hundred Years War?

4 is now the home of the writer of *Harry Potter*?

5 had a queen called Mary who was beheaded in England?

6 sent a fleet of ships to invade England?

7 fought a War of Independence against England in 1857?

8 in the United Kingdom does not have its flag as part of the Union Flag?

This reader uses the **EXPANSIVE READING** approach, where the text becomes a springboard to improve language skills and to explore historical background, cultural connections and other topics suggested by the text.
The new structures introduced in this step of our **R**EADING & **T**RAINING series are listed below. Naturally, structures from lower steps are included too. For a complete list of structures used over all the six steps, see *The Black Cat Guide to Graded Readers*, which is also downloadable at no cost from our website, blackcat-cideb.com.
The vocabulary used at each step is carefully checked against vocabulary lists used for internationally recognised examinations.

Step **Two B1.1**

All the structures used in the previous levels, plus the following:

Verb tenses

Present Perfect Simple: indefinite past with *yet*, *already*, *still*; recent past with *just*; past action leading to present situation

Past Perfect Simple: in reported speech

Verb forms and patterns

Regular verbs and most irregular verbs

Passive forms with *going to* and *will*

So / neither / nor + auxiliaries in short answers

Question tags (in verb tenses used so far)

Verb + object + full infinitive (e.g. *I want you to help*)

Reported statements with *say* and *tell*

Modal verbs

Can't: logical necessity

Could: possibility

May: permission

Might (present and future reference): possibility; permission

Must: logical necessity

Don't have to / haven't got to: lack of obligation

Don't need to / needn't: lack of necessity

Types of clause

Time clauses introduced by *when*, *while*, *until*, *before*, *after*, *as soon as*

Clauses of purpose: *so that*; *(in order) to* (infinitive of purpose)